D0192133

# ROASTS

30130 148841496

RYLAND
PETERS
& SMALL

LONDON NEW YORK

# ROASTS

meat, fish, vegetables, sauces and more

**Sonia Stevenson** photography by Martin Brigdale

First published in hardback
in Great Britain in 2004

This paperback edition published in 2007
by Ryland Peters & Small
20–21 Jockey's Fields
London WC1R 4BW
www.rylandpeters.com

10 9 8 7 6 5 4 3 2 1

Text © Sonia Stevenson 2004, 2007
Design and photographs
© Ryland Peters & Small 2004, 2007

Printed in China

The author's moral rights have been
asserted. All rights reserved. No part of this
publication may be reproduced, stored in a
retrieval system or transmitted in any form
or by any means, electronic, mechanical,
photocopying or otherwise, without the prior
permission of the publisher.

ISBN-13: 978 1 84597 544 9
ISBN-10: 1 84597 544 8

A CIP record for this book is available
from the British Library.

**Dedication**
To Roy Wilton, who has, so many times and
so patiently, helped me through the maze of
butchery with his expert advice.

**Author's Acknowledgements**
My thanks, as usual and primarily to my
editor, Elsa Petersen-Schepelern, my agent
Fiona Lindsay and Limelight, then to all my
friends and family who help with advice and
are my guinea pigs.

**Publisher's Acknowledgements**
Our thanks to Brian Bailey of A. Dove & Son,
Butchers, of Northcote Road, Battersea,
London SW11, for his ongoing technical
advice.
Recipe for Garlic with Goat Cheese, page 31,
© Elsa Petersen-Schepelern

**Senior Designer** Steve Painter
**Commissioning Editor**
Elsa Petersen-Schepelern
**Production** Deborah Wehner
**Art Director** Gabriella Le Grazie
**Publishing Director** Alison Starling

**Food Stylist** Linda Tubby
**Prop Stylist** Helen Trent
**Indexer** Hilary Bird

All photography by Martin Brigdale except
page 5, 120 (left), 122, 127, 133 (top), 135
(top left) Peter Cassidy and page 121 left
William Lingwood.

**Notes**
• All spoon measurements are level unless
otherwise stated.
• All herbs are freshunless otherwise stated.
• Ingredients in this book are available from
larger supermarkets and gourmet stores.
See pages 141–2 for web and mail order
sources.
• Ovens should be preheated to the
specified temperature. Oven thermostats
are often wrong, so have yours tested and
calibrated if necessary. Oven thermometers
are available in kitchen shops and
department stores.
• An instant-read meat thermometer,
especially the small fountain-pen sized
versions used by professional chefs, are very
useful. See pages 141–2 for web and mail
order sources.

## Essex County Council Libraries

# contents

# warm, convivial, family food ...

A roast is always special. It makes a warm, convivial meal that's perfect for family get-togethers on weekends – or for special occasions, like Christmas, birthdays or anniversaries. It's the sort of meal that memories are made of – how many people remember fondly the roast their mothers cooked for Sunday lunch?

It's a very Western form of cooking. The domestic oven was developed in the nineteenth century. Before that, except for the huge spits found in big houses, most family cooking was done in a pot over an open fire. The roasting oven, with its ability to control temperature, albeit in a very primitive way, meant that the roast gradually became the quintessential family meal. Carving was very much a job for the head of the house and the skill was passed down from father to son, as is still the case with some families.

Several factors combine to make roasting one of the most delicious forms of cooking and, because there is endless opportunity for variety, everyone has their own opinion of what makes a perfect roast and how to achieve it, even though one person's preference may not be another's. It is sad that in these days of modern technology the open fire is no longer an option for most households. Our restaurant had a spit that had to be wound up every fifteen minutes by the customers, who took great pleasure in cooking their own Sunday roast in front of the huge log fire.

Almost any food, be it fish, flesh, fowl or vegetable can be roasted and each has its own idiosyncrasies. Such variety could be confusing, but one observation links them all – without doubt, the better the quality of the raw ingredient, the better the roast will be, and this is vitally important since roasting brings out and exposes the best and worst in food.

You need an even source of heat that can be readily altered to accommodate the different styles of roasting. Our modern ovens, often fan-assisted to keep the air and heat circulating more evenly around the meat, have all the safeguards that our foremothers lacked. Originally, the open fire must have contributed to many disasters. From personal experience, I can say it is often a hit and miss affair, although a happy challenge occasionally.

Some people say that roasting is expensive, and the fast-roasting method using tender cuts does shrink the size of the roast. However, this does not mean that it is only possible to choose from the most expensive cuts. Slow-roasting uses inexpensive, tougher cuts and produces succulent texture. As well as using this method for meat, roasting a Christmas turkey overnight in a gentle oven can take a lot of the stress out of family gatherings.

From a health point of view, in my opinion, it's a good way to cook. More fat comes out of a roast than is ever used to cook it, and you pour most of it away.

Roasting vegetables has become more and more popular, not only for people with health considerations or for vegetarians, but also for the family cook wanting another option to the 'boiled to death' vegetable matter which was, many times, inadvertently imposed on my family when a timing went wrong. This method concentrates the taste of the vegetables and gives them a unique flavour, similar to that achieved on an outdoor barbecue.

Roasting is the best way to cook fish – it retains all the juices, keeps smells to a minimum, concentrates the flavour and makes serving easy. I well remember a fateful day when I was poaching a large salmon, but had forgotten to use the metal strainer for lifting out the fish. In my efforts to drain off the water, the salmon was tipped out as well, the head fell off and the rest broke in several pieces and had to be served in a dish with the sauce poured over to hide the disaster. After that, poaching has been a thing of the past and roasting has taken over.

A method as basic as roasting is really simplicity in itself and with quality ingredients, a good source of steady heat and a book of recipes, how can you fail?

vegetables

Individual squash filled with a vegetable stuffing make a light supper dish or a vegetarian starter. They can be prepared in advance and finished for the last 40 minutes at a later time.

# stuffed baby squash
## with ginger vinaigrette

6 small round squash, about 250 g each

sea salt and freshly ground black pepper

olive oil, for brushing

**stuffing**

4 red peppers

2 red onions, sliced

2 medium mushrooms, sliced

4 tomatoes, halved

2 tablespoons olive oil

sea salt and freshly ground black pepper

**ginger vinaigrette**

1 tablespoon vinegar

1 tablespoon olive oil

2 garlic cloves, crushed

3 cm fresh ginger, peeled and grated

½ teaspoon salt

**serves 6**

Cut the tops off the squash to use as lids. Set aside. Scoop out and discard the seeds, season the cavity and let drain upside down.

To make the stuffing, halve and deseed the peppers, then cut into 1 cm cubes. Put the peppers, onions, mushrooms and tomatoes in a roasting tin and sprinkle with the olive oil, salt and pepper. Roast in a preheated oven at 200°C (400°F) Gas 6 for 30 minutes to dry and char them a little. Turn them over from time to time so they cook evenly.

To make the vinaigrette, mix the vinegar, olive oil, garlic, ginger and salt in a bowl, then pour over the vegetables and roast for 10 minutes.

Spoon the mixture into the squash, top with the lids, brush them with a little olive oil and return to the oven for a further 30–40 minutes, or until cooked through.

**Arguably the best-tasting squash and deep gold when roasted, butternut squash is an ideal accompaniment to so many dishes. If you roast it at a high heat, it will brown like a potato, or when cooked more gently, it marries well with fresh herbs.**

# roast butternut squash

1 large butternut squash or 2 small ones

2 tablespoons olive oil

75 g unsalted butter

a bunch of fresh thyme, tips snipped into sprigs

2 garlic cloves, sliced

sea salt and freshly ground black pepper

**serves 4–8**

Cut the squash in half lengthways and scoop out the seeds and pith with a spoon. Cut each half into 3–4 wedges, according to the size of the squash. There is no need to peel them.

Put the oil and butter in a roasting tin and heat on top of the stove until melted. Add the wedges of butternut and baste the pieces, turning them carefully to cover. Push the sprigs of thyme and slices of garlic between the wedges and sprinkle with salt and pepper.

Roast in a preheated oven at 190°C (375°F) Gas 5 for 30 minutes, turning the pieces over a couple of times to brown them lightly as they finish cooking.

**Variation**  Peel the wedges of butternut with a potato peeler or turning knife. Bring a large saucepan of salted water to the boil, add the wedges, return to the boil and simmer for about 5 minutes. Drain well. This initial par-boiling seasons them with salt and and gives a crunchy exterior.

**It is a pity that so often this vegetable is just plainly boiled. Properly blanched for a short while, then roasted in butter, it is transformed into a perfect accompaniment for any roast, especially fish.**

# fennel roasted in butter

3 bulbs of Florence fennel

4 tablespoons olive oil or melted butter

sea salt

chopped dill, tarragon
or fennel fronds (optional), to serve

**serves 6**

Trim and remove the stalks and coarse outer leaves from the fennel if necessary. Cut each bulb in half, then each half into 2–3 pieces, depending on size. Slice each piece with a bit of stem or root attached to keep the pieces in place. Reserve any feathery fronds, to chop over the dish just before serving.

Put the fennel in a large saucepan of lightly salted water, bring to the boil and blanch until nearly tender. Drain and pat dry.

Arrange the pieces in a single layer in a roasting tin, baste with the oil or butter and cook in a preheated oven at 220°C (425°F) Gas 7 for about 20 minutes. From time to time, turn them and baste with the oil or butter so they brown evenly on all sides.

To enhance the aniseed flavour, dust with chopped dill, tarragon or fennel fronds, if using, then serve.

**Variation** Sprinkle with cheese and cook a further 5 minutes, then serve as a separate dish or starter.

# roast potatoes

Potatoes are the quintessential roasted vegetable. Though new potatoes are used for roasting, the traditional choice is an old, floury potato, such as Maris Piper or King Edward. The idea is to get a crisp, crunchy outside and a fluffy inside.

• Potatoes can be roasted, either peeled or unpeeled.

• They are often par-boiled first. This gives them a fluffier interior and crisper exterior.

• If you score the outside of the potato first with a fork, they will be extra crunchy.

• The roasting fat used depends on what part of the world you live in. In some areas, it's olive oil (and increasingly so everywhere, as people get more health-conscious). In much of France and Scandinavia, it is butter. In south-west France, it is often delicious goose fat and duck fat, which undoubtedly give the best flavour.

150 ml double cream

½ teaspoon hot dry mustard

½ teaspoon salt

500 g potatoes, peeled and halved

**serves 4**

### Potatoes roasted in cream (right)
Put the cream, mustard and salt in a measuring jug and beat with a fork. Put the potatoes in a small roasting tin and pour the cream mixture over the top. Roast in a preheated oven at 180°C (350°F) Gas 4 for 1 hour, basting every 20 minutes. Serve with roast meat or poultry. The cream becomes buttery as it cooks – don't worry, it's going to turn brown and crumbly.

8 thick slices smoked streaky bacon, cut into squares

2 tablespoons olive oil

3 garlic cloves, sliced (optional)

500 g new potatoes, unpeeled, cut into 1 cm chunks

sea salt and freshly ground black pepper

1 tablespoon sliced spring onion tops, to serve

**serves 4**

### Roast potatoes with bacon and garlic
Put the bacon in a roasting tin, pour over the oil and toss to coat. Roast in a preheated oven at 190°C (375°F) Gas 5 for 5 minutes, adding the garlic, if using, after 3 minutes. Add the potatoes and toss to coat with the oil. Season with salt and pepper and roast for 30 minutes, stirring every 10 minutes. Serve sprinkled with the sliced spring onion tops.

A spectacular recipe from Sweden and one of the crunchiest ways to roast potatoes. It was invented in a Stockholm restaurant, Hasselbacken, which is still open today. It is delicious in that it provides multiple surfaces to become crisp. I have also seen it cooked with fresh bay leaves pressed into the slits (just tell your guests to remove them before eating – bay leaves are wonderful for flavouring, but not for eating).

# hasselback potatoes

6 medium roasting potatoes

4 tablespoons butter or goose fat, melted

2 tablespoons sieved and toasted breadcrumbs*

1 tablespoon freshly grated Parmesan cheese

sea salt and freshly ground black pepper

**serves 6**

Peel the potatoes and slice a thin sliver off each base to make the potato sit steady. Stick a skewer through each one, parallel to the work surface and about 1 cm from the base – this will prevent the knife from cutting right through the potato. Cut and slice the potatoes downwards towards the skewer, then remove the skewer. Soak and rinse them in several changes of water to remove the starch, which would stick the slices together.

Season with salt and pepper and sit them in a roasting tin in a preheated oven at 220°C (425°F) Gas 7 to dry off for 2 minutes, then baste with the melted butter.

Return the potatoes to the oven, basting several more times during the cooking until they are brown and crisp, about 1 hour.

**Variation** Sprinkle with breadcrumbs or cheese at least 30 minutes before the end of the cooking time.

* To make dried breadcrumbs, remove the crusts from a loaf of white bread and pulverize the rest in a blender. Spread the crumbs on a baking tray and toast in a preheated oven at 250°F (475°F) Gas 9 for 5 minutes until brown on top. Turn them over to expose the white crumb and continue toasting until dry and lightly brown all over. This will take several turns. Shake them through a coarse sieve and discard any residual crumb. Pour into a plastic bag, seal and store in the freezer.

# sweet potatoes en brochette

**These look rather like hasselback potatoes, except they are skewered right through the centre, then cut around to free each slice, leaving the skewer in place. This browns the slices individually without letting them fall to pieces in the pan. At the same time, they pick up lots of flavour from the roast.**

6 smallish sweet potatoes

fat from around the roast
or 3 tablespoons goose fat or butter

sea salt and freshly ground black pepper

6 metal skewers

**serves 6**

Peel the sweet potatoes and skewer each one lengthways through the centre. Slice them around the skewer and separate the rounds.

Arrange them around the bird or meat or in the roasting tin, baste generously with the cooking juices, goose fat or butter and season lightly with salt and pepper.

Roast in a preheated oven at 220°C (425°F) Gas 7 for 45 minutes or until browned – continue to baste them from time to time to prevent them from drying out.

# candied yams

**Sweet potatoes are often called yams in the US, and candied yams are a traditional American holiday dish. Sweet potatoes are different in different parts of the world – some are orange-fleshed and sweet, while others have purple skins and white dense flesh, rather like chestnuts.**

6 sweet potatoes

110 g butter, cut into pieces

200 g brown sugar

2 tablespoons real vanilla extract

**serves 6**

Boil the sweet potatoes in their skins until about half done, about 20 minutes. Drain, remove the skins, and slice lengthways. Arrange in a small, greased roasting tin and dot with the pieces of butter.

Put the brown sugar, vanilla and 50 ml water in a saucepan and bring to the boil to make a syrup. Pour over the sweet potatoes and roast in a preheated oven at 180°C (350°F) Gas 4 for 45–50 minutes, basting frequently with the syrup.

When roasted, the flavour of tomatoes becomes more intense because the moisture dries out in the oven. Even so, the better the quality of the tomato to begin with, the better the final dish will be. So buy the Italian varieties, which are often peculiar shapes, but have an extra something when it comes to flavour (what does shape matter when you've been dried out?)

# crunchy roast garlic tomatoes

4 large Italian tomatoes

1 teaspoon sugar

4 tablespoons olive oil

25 g fresh breadcrumbs

1 garlic clove, crushed

1 tablespoon chopped fresh flat leaf parsley

sea salt

**serves 4**

Slice the tomatoes in half around the 'equator'. Set them in a roasting dish, sprinkle with the sugar, salt and a trickle of the oil and roast in a preheated oven at 180°C (350°F) Gas 4 for 2 hours until nearly dried out.

Meanwhile, heat the rest of the oil in a frying pan, add the breadcrumbs and, when they start to brown, add the garlic and parsley. When they are lightly brown all over, strain off the excess oil through a sieve and sprinkle the crumbs over the tomatoes.

When ready to serve, reheat them in a preheated oven at 200°C (400°F) Gas 6 for 15–20 minutes.

Be sure to use a sweet eating apple for this recipe. The cooking variety turns to a purée and spoils the roasting effect. Celeriac must be thickly peeled to remove the tough outer skin. Choose young celeriac, because older ones develop a soft, spongy centre, unlike parsnips, which develop woody cores. Ideally, the centres of both vegetables should be cut away before cooking.

# roast apples
# and celeriac or parsnips

2 tablespoons olive oil

½ teaspoon dried sage

½ teaspoon salt

1 eating apple, cut into wedges

1 celeriac or 2 parsnips, about 350 g, peeled and cut into wedges

1 tablespoon chopped fresh flat leaf parsley

*a baking tray*

**serves 4**

Put the oil, sage and salt in a plastic bag, then add the apple and celeriac or parsnips. Roll them around until well coated with oil. Empty the bag onto a baking tray and roast in a preheated oven at 220°C (425°F) Gas 7 for 30 minutes, turning the vegetables every 10 minutes. Sprinkle with parsley, mix well and serve.

**Variations**

**Parsnip crisps**
Slice 500 g parsnips into thin rounds and coat with olive oil, salt and pepper. Spread them out on a baking tray and roast until brown and crisp. Serve with any roast, especially game.

**Roast parsnips**
To make one of the traditional accompaniments for roast beef (page 82), peel 500 g parsnips, then cut lengthways into halves or quarters, depending on size. Roast beside the beef for 1–1½ hours or until they develop a caramelized, roasted finish.

**So often carrots are used as part of a stew. For them to stand out as a vegetable dish, a little extra attention will make them something special. This treatment makes them sweet and glistening.**

# glazed roast carrots

750 g young carrots

1 tablespoon olive oil

50 g unsalted butter

1 teaspoon sugar

125 ml Madeira wine

sea salt and freshly ground black pepper

a handful of flat leaf parsley, coarsely chopped, to serve

**serves 4–6**

Wash and trim the carrots. If large, cut into 4 cm chunks, but if small or medium, leave them whole. Par-boil them in a large saucepan of boiling water for about 10 minutes, leaving them still slightly hard in the middle. Drain.

Meanwhile, heat the oil and butter in a roasting tin in a preheated oven at 200°C (400°F) Gas 6 until the butter begins to brown. Add the carrots, turn to coat in the oil, then sprinkle with salt, pepper and the sugar and return to the oven for 10 minutes. Turn them and roast for a further 15 minutes. Add the Madeira and cook until all the liquid has gone. Serve sprinkled with parsley.

**Variation**

**Roast carrots with honey and lemon glaze**
To make the honey and lemon glaze, put 2 tablespoons honey or sugar in a pan, add 2 tablespoons water, 2 teaspoons lemon juice and 10 g butter or 2 teaspoons olive oil. Bring to the boil and simmer for 1 minute to make a light syrup. Start the recipe as above, but pour over the honey and lemon glaze instead of the Madeira. Roast for a further 15 minutes or until the sugar caramelizes. Serve sprinkled with chopped parsley.

**Big flat mushrooms are delicious roasted in the oven, and so are the wild ones with an extra touch of hazelnut oil added to the cooking medium. Serve them as a first course, as part of an antipasti selection or as an accompaniment to roast meats, especially beef.**

# roast mushrooms
## with olive oil and pine nuts

1 tablespoon pine nuts

8 portobello mushrooms, or a mixture with cèpes (porcini), about 350 g

1 tablespoon lemon juice

4 tablespoons olive oil

2 garlic cloves, crushed

sea salt and freshly ground black pepper

1 tablespoon chopped fresh flat leaf parsley, to serve

*a large baking tray*

**serves 4 as an accompaniment or 2 as a starter**

Put the pine nuts in a dry frying pan and cook over gentle heat until golden. Shake from time to time and watch them closely because they burn easily. When aromatic, remove them to a plate and set aside.

Wipe or gently brush the mushrooms with a pastry brush to remove any dust, but do not wash them unless absolutely necessary.

Put the lemon juice in a bowl and stir in 3 tablespoons water.

Put the oil, garlic, salt and pepper in a small jug or bowl and pour half of it over the base of a large baking tray.

Arrange the mushrooms on the tray, open side down, in one layer and brush the tops with the rest of the oil.

Roast in a preheated oven at 220°C (425°F) Gas 7 for 10 minutes, then turn them over with tongs. Brush the inside of the mushrooms with the diluted lemon juice and return them to the oven for a further 5 minutes.

Remove from the oven, sprinkle with the pine nuts and chopped parsley and serve.

You might think that whole roast heads of garlic would would taste a bit robust, but such long cooking renders the cloves sweet, soft and nutty. Press out the flesh and spread it on toasted croutes, then serve in soup, with stews, or with this summery salad.

# roast whole heads of garlic
## with goats' cheese and croutes

4 whole heads of garlic

olive oil, plus extra to serve

sea salt and freshly ground black pepper

**to serve**

bitter leaves, such as frisée, or peppery ones, such as rocket

8 slices goats' cheese, about 2 cm thick

lemon wedges

8 oven-toasted slices of baguette

**serves 8 as a starter**

Cut each head of garlic in half, then arrange in a single layer in a roasting tin. Spoon olive oil over the top and sprinkle with salt. Roast in a preheated oven at 200°C (400°F) Gas 6 for 45 minutes– 1 hour or until the cloves are very soft.

Serve on a bed of bitter leaves with a thick slice of goats' cheese, a wedge of lemon and an oven-toasted croute or slice of bread. Dress with olive oil and freshly ground black pepper. Guests press the garlic paste out of the papery peel and spread it on the croutes. Eat with the cheese and salad leaves.

**Variations**

**Individually roasted garlic cloves**
Arrange the peeled garlic cloves in an ovenproof dish, add 4 tablespoons olive oil and toss until well coated. Roast in a preheated oven at 180°C (350°F) Gas 4 for 30 minutes.

**Roast garlic with sugar and brandy**
Roast peeled garlic cloves as above for 30 minutes, then sprinkle with 4 tablespoons sugar and 4 tablespoons brandy. Return to the oven for another 30 minutes until they are crunchy.

These onions are meant to be served in their skins and the centres squeezed or spooned out by the guests. They make a wonderful antipasto, but if you are serving them as a side dish with lamb, insert a sprig of rosemary into the onions before roasting.

# roast onions

12 large red onions

4 tablespoons olive oil

sea salt and freshly ground black pepper

**herbed butter**

250 g unsalted butter, softened

4 tablespoons chopped fresh herbs, such as thyme, tarragon and/or chives

*kitchen foil*

**serves 6–12 as an antipasto**

To make the herbed butter, put the softened butter in a bowl and mash with a fork. Add the herbs and mash again. Use from the bowl, or chill a little, transfer to a sheet of kitchen foil and roll into a log. The log may be kept in the refrigerator or frozen for future use. You can cut off rounds to use with dishes such as pan-grilled steak or steamed vegetables.

To prepare the onions, leave their skins on, but take a small slice off each root and trim the ends so they will sit upright. Brush them all over with half the olive oil and cut each one from the top down towards the root without cutting right through. Give them a quarter turn and make a similar cut as before.

Pack them closely into a roasting tin so they sit upright. Open the cuts a little, pour ½ teaspoon of oil into each one, then sprinkle with salt and pepper.

Roast in a preheated oven at 190°C (375°F) Gas 5 for 1½ hours or until the centres are soft. Lift them onto individual plates and put a spoonful of herb butter into each one. Alternatively, pile into a serving dish for guests to help themselves.

**Variation** Put 4 tablespoons cider vinegar, 4 tablespoons honey, 2 crushed garlic cloves and 1 tablespoon raisins in a saucepan and simmer for 1 minute. Add this to the onions during the last 30 minutes of cooking time.

**The joy of this dish is that you need not stick to the same selection of vegetables as here. Mushrooms, new potatoes and carrots all roast well in a medley. You can also ring the changes with different herbs and spices. An endlessly adaptable dish.**

# roast summer vegetables

1 small aubergine, or 3–4 Japanese aubergines

4 small red onions

1 sweet potato

3 tablespoons olive oil

8 cherry tomatoes

2 peppers, red and/or yellow

2 medium courgettes or
1 small soft-skinned squash

1 whole head of garlic, separated
into cloves, but unpeeled

1–2 large sprigs of rosemary or thyme

sea salt and freshly ground black pepper

**serves 4**

Slice the aubergine into bite-sized wedges, quarter the onions, peel the sweet potato and cut it into chunks.

Put the aubergine, onions and sweet potato in a plastic bag, add the oil and shake gently until everything is well coated. Transfer them all to a roasting tin and sprinkle with salt. Add the tomatoes and turn to coat with the oil.

Roast in a preheated oven at 230°C (450°F) Gas 8 for 15 minutes while you prepare the other vegetables.

Remove the stalks from the peppers and the seeds and ribs from the inside. Slice the flesh into thick wedges or chunks. Trim the courgettes and cut them lengthways into quarters and again in half if they are too long. Deseed the squash and cut it into chunks.

Add the peppers and courgettes to the roasting tin, turning them all in the oil. Tuck in the garlic and rosemary and return the tin to the oven for another 15 minutes. Lower the oven temperature to 180°C (350°F) Gas 4 and cover the tin with foil. Remove the foil after 15 minutes. If there is too much liquid in the tin, continue roasting uncovered for a final 10 minutes or so.

Serve as an antipasto, as an accompaniment to roast meats, or with chunky bread and other dishes as a light lunch.

**fish**

**Roasting brings out the best in sea bass, firming up the flesh and concentrating its flavour. Because it is now farmed, there should be no shortage of this splendid fish – small, one-portion bass should always be available. However, the dish is even better if you can find a large, 2 kg wild one. This vivid sauce may be made in advance – serve it separately in a jug or bowl.**

# marinated sea bass
## with paprika and spices

1 large (2 kg) or 4 small (500 g each) sea bass, scaled and cleaned

sea salt and freshly ground black pepper

**marinade**

freshly squeezed juice of 2 lemons

2 tablespoons olive oil

½ teaspoon ground cumin

1 teaspoon sweet oak-smoked paprika

**sauce**

2 red peppers

2 tablespoons olive oil

½ teaspoon cumin

1 teaspoon sweet oak-smoked paprika

1 garlic clove, crushed

8 medium tomatoes, skinned, deseeded and chopped

a pinch of saffron threads, infused in 125 ml boiling water

125 ml red wine vinegar

1 teaspoon salt

1 teaspoon sugar

1 tablespoon chopped fresh flat leaf parsley

*a baking tray, covered with non-stick baking parchment*

*an instant-read thermometer*

**serves 4**

To make the marinade, put the lemon juice, olive oil, cumin and paprika in a bowl and beat with a fork.

Cover the baking tray with non-stick parchment, to act as a cradle when you are ready to lift the fish onto a serving dish.

Cut off the fins, check the cavities and rinse out only if necessary. Pat dry with kitchen paper, then brush the cavities with some of the marinade and reserve the rest. Put the fish on the parchment, cover with a damp cloth and leave for 2 hours in a cool place.

Meanwhile, to make the sauce, roast the peppers in a preheated oven at 220°C (425°F) Gas 7 until the skins start to char and they can be peeled. Remove from the heat, remove the skins, pull out the stalks and discard the seeds and white membrane. Cut the flesh into small chunks and set aside.

Heat the remaining marinade in a small pan, add the oil, cumin, paprika and garlic and cook gently for a couple of minutes until aromatic. Add the tomatoes, saffron, vinegar, salt and sugar and cook to a purée. Add the peppers and parsley and reheat thoroughly, without boiling, otherwise the sauce will lose some of its freshness.

Season the fish with salt and pepper, put it (still in its parchment cradle) in a roasting tin and cook in a preheated oven at 220°C (425°F) Gas 7 for 25–30 minutes or until an instant-read thermometer registers 58°C (136°F) at the thickest part of the back. Smaller fish will take about 20 minutes. Transfer to a large dish, remove the parchment and serve the sauce in a small jug.

# oven-roasted red snapper
## with sorrel and salsa verde

4 red snapper, about 500 g each,
scaled and cleaned

100 g unsalted butter

24 sorrel leaves

sea salt and freshly ground black pepper

Salsa Verde (page 121), to serve

*a baking tray, buttered*

*an instant-read thermometer*

**serves 4**

**This recipe may be used with any round fish, but preferably not an oily variety. The sorrel is not essential, but it does supply a lemony seasoning for the dish. Serve with roast tomatoes (page 23) and new potatoes.**

Make sure the fish have been well scaled – snapper have very large scales that can be unpleasant if you bite into one.

Cut off the heads, if preferred, season the cavities with salt and pepper, then butter very well. Arrange the sorrel on the buttered baking tray and put the fish on top. Lay some more leaves over the fish and roast them in a preheated oven at 250°C (500°F) Gas 9 for 8 minutes. Turn them over and cook for a further 8 minutes, or until an instant-read thermometer registers 58°C (136°F).

Remove the fish from the oven and transfer to heated dinner plates. Warm the salsa verde and trickle over the fish.

**Tuna is a dark-fleshed fish that needs extra flavouring and takes well to hot paprika seasoning. The topping gives a moist and crunchy texture to a fish that can become dry and overcooked only too easily. Serve on a bed of buttered spinach with romesco sauce – a hot, pungent, Catalan sauce thickened with ground almonds and hazelnuts, which is often served with fish and can also be used as a dip for crudités.**

# tuna with paprika crumbs
## and romesco sauce

To make the paprika topping, put the oil in a frying pan, add the breadcrumbs, basil, paprika, tomato paste, sugar and salt. Stir well and fry until crunchy. Remove from the pan and let cool.

Season the tuna with salt and pepper, put on the oiled baking tray and roast in a preheated oven at 250°C (500°F) Gas 9 for 5 minutes.

Remove from the oven and turn over the steaks. Pile the paprika breadcrumbs on top, then add the slice of cheese. Return to the oven and cook for a further 5 minutes or until the cheese has melted. Serve on a bed of buttered spinach, with romesco sauce served separately.

4 tuna steaks, 175 g each

40 g Cheddar cheese, cut into 4 thin slices

sea salt and freshly ground black pepper

**paprika breadcrumb crunch**

1 tablespoon olive oil

50 g fresh white breadcrumbs

1 tablespoon chopped fresh basil

½ teaspoon hot oak-smoked paprika

1 teaspoon tomato paste

½ teaspoon sugar

½ teaspoon salt

**to serve**

buttered spinach

Romesco Sauce (page 121)

*a baking tray, oiled*

**serves 4**

Years ago, one of the most popular ways to cook salmon was to poach it either as cutlets or whole. However, now that salmon is more often filleted, the best way to cook it is to roast skin side up, then peel off the skin and scales as soon as it is cooked. This way, there is no messy draining of the fish and less chance of overcooking it – salmon being one fish that's best served slightly rare. If you cannot easily get sorrel, season the sauce with lemon juice instead.

# roast salmon fillets
## with sorrel sauce

4 salmon fillets or tranches, about 175 g each

3 tablespoons plain flour, seasoned with salt and pepper

unsalted butter, for roasting

**sorrel sauce**

125 g unsalted butter

60 g sorrel

3 egg yolks

sea salt and freshly ground black pepper

**to serve**

Fennel Roasted in Butter (page 15)

boiled new potatoes

*a baking tray, well buttered*

**serves 4**

Heat the buttered baking tray in a preheated oven at 230°C (450°F) Gas 8. Dust the fillets with the flour and put them skin side up on the sheet. Roast for 6–8 minutes. Test for doneness by trying to remove the skin – if it comes off, the fish is ready.

Remove from the oven, then carefully peel off the skin and discard it. Keep the fish warm.

To make the sorrel sauce, put the butter in a saucepan and heat until it begins to froth. Add the sorrel and simmer until it turns a khaki colour. Put the egg yolks in a blender, add 2 tablespoons water and blend until fluffy. Reduce the speed and pour all the sorrel and butter into the egg mixture with the machine running. Taste and adjust the seasoning with salt and pepper.

Spoon pools of sauce onto 4 heated dinner plates. Turn the fillets over onto the sauce and serve with roast fennel and new potatoes.

**A very versatile dish, this can be served just as it is or made into a special-occasion, all-in-one dish with one of the sauces. Prepared in advance, it needs only to be roasted, basted and served for an effortless supper.**

6 cod cutlets, 250 g each for a main course, 200 g as a starter

about 2 tablespoons unsalted butter

freshly grated nutmeg

6 lemon slices

2 large potatoes, par-boiled in salted water and cut into walnut-sized pieces

sea salt and freshly ground black pepper

**base of thyme and lemon**

175 g unsalted butter

2 onions, chopped

2 garlic cloves, crushed

1 teaspoon fresh lemon thyme leaves

6 peppercorns

2 bay leaves

**to serve (optional)**

tomato sauce, such as Romesco (page 121)

herb sauce, such as Sorrel Sauce (page 44)

Fennel Roasted in Butter (page 15)

**serves 6**

# roast cod cutlets
## on a base of thyme and lemon

Season the cutlets with sea salt and freshly ground black pepper.

To make the base of thyme and lemon, heat the 175 g butter in a frying pan, add the onions, garlic, thyme, peppercorns and bay leaves and cook gently until softened but not browned.

Spread the mixture in a roasting tin. Put the cutlets on top, with about 1 teaspoon of the butter on each piece. Add the nutmeg and lemon slices. Tuck the potato pieces around. Roast in a preheated oven at 190°C (375°F) Gas 5 for 35 minutes, basting once with the juices from the lemon slices.

Serve as it is, or with a tomato or herb sauce and roast fennel.

**This is usually made with a whole, large monkfish tail but cutlets or even four individual tails may be used instead. Adding cream to the Niçoise sauce makes an unusual variation, while black olives and fennel fronds add colour to the dish. Serve on a bed of rice.**

# roast gigot of monkfish
## with sauce niçoise

1 kg monkfish tail

sea salt and freshly ground black pepper

olive oil, for brushing

**niçoise sauce**

200 g canned tomatoes or 6 fresh tomatoes, skinned and deseeded

2 garlic cloves, crushed

2 tablespoons olive oil

125 ml white wine

250 ml fish stock

leaves from 2–3 sprigs of thyme, chopped

leaves from 2–3 small sprigs of tarragon, chopped

2 fresh sage leaves

1 bay leaf

sea salt and freshly ground black pepper

**to serve**

12 black olives, chopped

fennel fronds

*an instant-read thermometer*

**serves 4**

To make the Niçoise sauce, put the tomatoes, garlic and oil in a saucepan, bring to the boil, reduce the heat and simmer until they cook to a pulp – crush them from time to time. Add the wine and keep simmering until it has been absorbed by the tomatoes. Add the stock, thyme, tarragon, sage, bay leaf, salt and pepper.

Peel the skin off the monkfish and cut away the loose membrane. Shorten the tail with scissors but do not cut into the flesh or it will shrink back and expose the bone as it cooks. Brush the fish with the oil and season with salt and pepper.

Spoon half the sauce into a roasting tin, rest the fish on it and roast in a preheated oven at 180°C (350°F) Gas 4 for 10 minutes. Turn the fish over and continue to cook until an instant-read thermometer registers 58°C (136°F), about 10 minutes. Transfer the fish to a serving dish and keep it warm.

Pour the roasting juices back into the saucepan of Niçoise sauce, bring to the boil and simmer until reduced to a pulp. Add salt and pepper to taste.

Pour the sauce around the fish, add the olives and fennel fronds and serve.

**poultry and game**

Basting is the secret of a perfect roast. Basting with butter brings out the best flavour from the bird, but you can also use oil or goose fat, or add wine or herbs to the basting mixture. Whichever combination of ingredients you choose, the roasting technique is much the same.

When judging quantities, 500 g per person works out about right. So for six people you will need a 3 kg bird. Adding stuffing is the best way to extend the number of helpings and it also adds another twist to the dish. Recently, stuffing the cavity of the chicken has fallen from favour on food-safety grounds and it is recommended that you stuff the neck instead. However, it is up to you. If you like, you can cook the stuffing separately in a baking dish (note, page 117). This amount of stuffing is enough for a large chicken or small turkey.

# italian roast chicken
## with salami stuffing

1 garlic clove, halved (optional)

1 whole chicken, 3 kg

Salami Stuffing (page 118)

50 g unsalted butter

2 tablespoons olive oil

75 ml Italian white wine, such as Orvieto Secco

250 ml strong chicken stock

freshly grated zest of 1 unwaxed lemon

1 teaspoon chopped fresh flat leaf parsley

sea salt and freshly ground black pepper

*an instant-read thermometer*

**serves 6**

If using garlic, rub the cut surface over the skin of the bird and put the rest inside the cavity. Add the stuffing to the bird from the neck end and fold the skin over, skewering it closed underneath.

Meanwhile, melt the butter in a saucepan with the oil, salt and pepper and use to brush the bird inside and out. Set the bird on its side in a shallow roasting tin and roast in a preheated oven at 200°C (400°F) Gas 6 for 15 minutes. Baste with the melted butter mixture again, then turn it over onto its other side, baste again and roast for another 15 minutes. Finally, turn it on its back and, basting frequently, about every 15 minutes, continue to roast until an instant-read thermometer* registers 82°C (180°F) at the thickest part of the leg – with a big bird, this will take at least 1½ hours. Transfer the chicken to a serving platter.

To make the gravy, put the tin on top of the stove, add the wine, bring to the boil and reduce by half. Add the stock and reduce by half again. Add the lemon zest, parsley and salt and pepper to taste, then serve separately.

* If you don't have an instant-read thermometer, test chicken and other poultry by inserting a skewer into the thickest part of the thigh. The juices should run clear and golden (press a metal spoon against the thigh to check the colour). If there is any trace of blood, return to the oven and cook longer until the juices are clear.

**These little birds are easy to serve at a dinner when there is not much time for cooking. They take just over thirty minutes in the oven, and the juices make a delicious and simple gravy. Serve with potatoes and a simple fresh salad.**

# spatchcocked poussins
## with rosemary and lemon glaze

4–6 poussins

1 tablespoon freshly squeezed lemon juice

250 ml chicken stock (optional)

1 tablespoon unsalted butter

1 tablespoon chopped fresh flat leaf parsley

sea salt and freshly ground black pepper

**marinade**

30 g unsalted butter

2 tablespoons extra virgin olive oil

2 teaspoons freshly grated lemon zest

a sprig of rosemary

2 garlic cloves, sliced

75 ml white wine

**serves 4–6**

To prepare the marinade, put the butter, olive oil, lemon zest, rosemary, garlic and wine in a saucepan and bring to the boil. Remove from the heat and let cool.

Put each bird breast side down on a work surface. Using kitchen scissors, cut along either side of the backbones and remove them.

Put the bones in a large saucepan, cover with cold water, bring to the boil and simmer for 30 minutes. Lift out the bones with tongs and boil down the stock to about 250 ml. Set aside.*

Meanwhile, turn the birds breast side up and flatten the breastbones until you hear them crack. Flatten the birds further, folding the legs inward. Set them side-by-side in a roasting tin and sprinkle with salt and pepper. Pour over the marinade and transfer the tin to the refrigerator until 30 minutes or so before you start to cook.

Roast in the middle of a preheated oven at 240°C (475°F) Gas 8 for 35 minutes. Baste the birds with the juices after 20 minutes. When they are cooked, lift them onto a serving dish, stir the lemon juice into the pan juices, then stir in the stock, butter and parsley. Taste and adjust the seasoning with salt and pepper, then serve.

* When available, I always use the bones of a roast to make stock. Feel free to use the fresh stock now sold in supermarkets if that is more convenient for you.

This makes a moist, spicy dish for a light lunch. If you would like a more fiery taste, increase the quantity of chillies and use hot paprika. This dish would also be delicious served with tacos for lunch or a picnic. Just reduce the gravy juices to make a concentrated sauce and serve with plenty of crunchy green salad.

# sonoran spiced orange chicken

1 chicken, about 1.5 kg

1 tablespoon olive oil

2 teaspoons sweet oak-smoked paprika

½ teaspoon crushed chilli flakes

2 teaspoons ground cumin

1 teaspoon ground cinnamon

1 tablespoon chopped fresh oregano or marjoram

1 unwaxed orange

1–2 tablespoons unsalted butter

sea salt and freshly ground black pepper

*an instant-read thermometer*

**serves 4**

Loosen the skin around the cavity of the bird and ease the skin away from the breast. Pour in ½ tablespoon of the oil and massage it around underneath the skin with your fingertips.

Put the paprika, chilli flakes, cumin, cinnamon and 1 teaspoon of the chopped oregano in a bowl, stir well, then push half the mixture under the skin of the chicken.

Cut 2 slices off the top of the orange and cut the rest in quarters. Push the slices under the skin on each side of the breast. Rub the outside of the bird with the remaining oil and spices. Put the butter, the remaining herbs, the orange quarters, salt, pepper and 2 tablespoons water in the cavity.

Put the bird in a roasting tin and roast in the middle of a preheated oven at 170°C (325°F) Gas 3 for 1½ hours, basting from time to time, until an instant-read thermometer registers 82°C (180°F) at the thickest part of the leg.

To serve, remove the bird from the oven and pour the juices out of the cavity into the tin – squeeze the juice from the orange quarters and discard the skins. Stir the juices and spoon them over the chicken when it is dished up.

Carve the meat in thickish slices, giving everyone a bit of the skin and a spoonful of the juice.

**This is one of my favourite recipes. It can be so easily varied with other ingredients – try marinating the chicken in some curry paste or just add olives and gherkins to the cook-in sauce. Serve it with spinach or any other green vegetable. Croutes of fried bread are a traditional French accompaniment. Wicked but delicious.**

# quick-roasted chicken pieces
## with tomatoes, mushrooms and brandy on crusty croutes

4 large chicken pieces, such as breasts or whole legs

1 teaspoon olive oil

**sauce**

100 g unsalted butter

1 teaspoon fresh thyme leaves

2 bay leaves

4 shallots

2 beef tomatoes, skinned and deseeded

250 g portobello mushrooms, sliced

100 ml brandy

sea salt and freshly ground black pepper

**crusty croutes (optional)**

4 slices white bread, crusts removed

3 tablespoons unsalted butter, or melted clarified butter

**serves 4**

Put the chicken pieces skin side down in a roasting tin, brush them with the oil and roast in a preheated oven at 220°C (425°F) Gas 7 for 10 minutes.

Meanwhile, to make the sauce, heat the butter in a frying pan, add the thyme, bay leaves and shallots and sauté until softened but not browned. Add the tomatoes and mushrooms and simmer until the liquid disappears and the tomato mixture starts to brown. Add the brandy, salt and pepper.

Remove the tin from the oven, turn the chicken pieces over, spoon the sauce around, then reduce the heat to 160°C (325°F) Gas 3 and return to the oven for 30 minutes.

Serve each piece of chicken on a square of crisp fried bread* and pile the savoury sauce around.

* To make the crusty croutes, spread the slices of bread generously with the butter and set on a metal tray in a preheated oven at 230°C (450°F) Gas 8 for 10 minutes or until golden brown. Turn once during cooking. Alternatively, you can dip them in melted clarified butter and fry on both sides in a hot pan until crisp. Drain on kitchen paper.

The salt crust is not for eating. It is there to contain all the juices and aromas – break it open just as you are about to serve. Take the chicken on a picnic, still in the crust, and it will still be hot and beautifully cooked, and spectacular when you break it open. A classic recipe.

# chicken in a salt crust

1 recipe Apricot Stuffing (page 117)

1 roasting chicken, about 2 kg

**salt crust**

250 g wholemeal plain flour

250 g coarse salt

200 ml water

**to serve**

Cranberry Relish (page 120)

boiled new potatoes

*a baking tray*

*an instant-read thermometer*

**serves 4**

To make the salt crust, put the flour, salt and water in a bowl and mix to a dough. Set aside.

Prepare the stuffing mixture and use to stuff the bird.

Break off about one-third of the dough and flatten it onto a baking tray. Put the bird on top, flatten pieces of the dough between your hands and cover the bird with it until none of the chicken is visible. Take particular care to join the top of the dough to the dough underneath.

Put the baking tray with the chicken in the middle of a preheated oven and cook at 220°C (425°F) Gas 7 for about 1½ hours or until an instant-read thermometer inserted through the dough into the thickest part of the thigh registers 82°C (180°F).

To serve, break open and discard the crust and transfer the chicken to a serving dish. Carve and serve with Cranberry Relish and new potatoes.

**Duck is a rich meat and sauerkraut make a perfect complement, both in flavour and goodness. Served with frankfurters and gammon, this becomes one of the traditional dishes of Alsace. It can be served with potatoes (roasted in duck fat if you have any).**

# roast duck à l'alsacienne
## with sauerkraut and frankfurters

1 jar sauerkraut, about 800 g

250 g streaky bacon or smoked pork hock, cut into chunks or slices

12 frankfurters

1 duck, about 3 kg

sea salt and freshly ground black pepper

*an instant-read thermometer*

**serves 6**

Empty the sauerkraut into a saucepan. Cover with boiling water and bring to the boil again. Drain, discarding the water (unless you like very strong sauerkraut) and top up again with more water, then bring to the boil. Add the pieces of bacon or hock and simmer for 80 minutes. When the sauerkraut is tender, drain off this water into another saucepan, add the frankfurters and reheat just before serving (they are already cooked). Put the sauerkraut aside.

Meanwhile, sprinkle the duck with salt and pepper and put in a roasting tin without any oil. Roast in a preheated oven at 200°C (400°F) Gas 6 for 1½ hours, first on one side for 30 minutes, then the other for 20 minutes and finally on its back, or until an instant-read thermometer registers 82°C (180°F) at the thickest part of the thigh.

Remove the duck from the oven and let rest for 10 minutes. Remove the bird from the roasting tin, draining any juices from the cavity back into the tin. Put the duck on a carving board, pull back the legs and cut off at the joints. Cut each one into thigh and drumstick. Slice off the breasts and cut each one in half. Put on a heatproof plate and keep them warm. Reserve the carcass to make a stock for another occasion.

Spoon off all but about 2 tablespoons of the fat from the roasting tin into a heatproof container and keep for another occasion. Add the drained sauerkraut to the fat in the tin and mix well. Pile it all onto a large serving dish, add the heated frankfurters and the pieces of duck with its juices, then serve.

For this dish, choose a breed of duck that is as lean as possible and save any fat rendered during cooking for roasting the potatoes. The breed will depend on where you live, but often will be one crossed with a wild or Barbary duck. For some reason, the Chinese seem to have a monopoly on the best ducks, so if you live near a Chinatown market, buy a fresh duck from there.

# roast duck with cherry salsa

1 duck, about 3 kg

250 ml fresh duck or chicken stock (see method)

salt (see method)

3 tablespoons clear honey

1 tablespoon red wine vinegar

500 g fresh cherries

1 recipe Cherry Salsa (page 121)

*a rack for the roasting tin (optional)*

*an instant-read thermometer*

**serves 4**

Trim off any loose fat and skin from the duck and make a stock with the giblets and wing tips.* Alternatively, use 250 ml ready-made stock. Prick the duck all over, especially around the thighs, to help release the fat during cooking. Dry with a cloth and rub with salt.

Put the duck on its side in a roasting tin and cook in a preheated oven at 250°C (500°F) Gas 9 for 20 minutes. Turn it onto its other side and cook for another 20 minutes, then lower the temperature to 180°C (350°F) Gas 4. Pour off the fat into a heatproof container, let cool, cover and keep in the refrigerator for future roasting.

To make a honey glaze, put the honey and vinegar in a small saucepan and bring to the boil. Boil for 30 seconds, remove from the heat and set aside.

If you are using a roasting rack, set it in the roasting tin. Put the duck on the rack on its back and roast for a further 40 minutes. Brush the duck with a layer of honey glaze and roast for another 20 minutes. Lift the duck onto a platter and transfer all the pan juices and fat to a saucepan.

Raise the oven temperature to 230°C (450°F) Gas 8. Brush the duck again with glaze, then return it to the oven. Cook for a further 20 minutes or until an instant-read thermometer registers 82°C (180°F) at the thickest part of the thigh.

To make a sauce, remove and discard the duck fat from the sediment in the saucepan, add the stock, taste and reduce if necessary. Serve with the duck and cherry salsa.

* To make a stock, put the giblets and wing tips in a saucepan, cover with cold water, bring to the boil, reduce the heat and simmer for 1 hour. Skim off the foam from time to time.

Family tradition will dictate the best way to present a festive turkey. I prefer to have two stuffings – one with fresh chestnuts for the neck cavity and the other a light herb and lemon bread stuffing made with plenty of butter, for the body cavity. It absorbs lots of juices and is fabulous served cold the next day. Give yourself a generous 40 minutes at the end for the turkey to keep warm and rest, while everything else is finished. See page 135 for general turkey-cooking preparation.

# roast turkey
## with lemon and herb stuffing

1 turkey, with giblets
1 onion, coarsely chopped
a sprig of thyme
1 bay leaf
125 g salted butter
sea salt and freshly ground black pepper
Lemon and Herb Stuffing (page 118)

**to serve**

Bacon Rolls (page 123)
Chipolatas (page 123)
Sausage Meat Patties (page 123)
Bread Sauce (page 118)
lightly boiled Brussels sprouts
Roast Potatoes (page 16)

*squares of muslin, paper or kitchen foil
(enough to cover the breast and drumsticks)*

**for sizes, serving quantities and
cooking times, see the chart on page 135**

To make a stock, the day before, put the giblets, minus the liver, but with the neck chopped in half, in a saucepan. Add the onion, thyme and bay leaf. Cover with water and bring slowly to the boil, removing any foam as it rises. Simmer for 2 hours and strain. Taste and, if necessary, reduce to strengthen the flavour.

Wipe out the neck area and cavity of the turkey with a damp cloth and lightly season the inside. Spoon in the chosen stuffings, allowing plenty of room for each one to expand. This is especially true for the neck stuffing.

Put half the butter in a saucepan and melt gently. Using your hands, spread the remaining butter all over the skin. Soak the muslin or paper in the melted butter and drape over the bird, with a double layer covering the drumsticks.

Preheat the oven to 180°C (350°F) Gas 4. Put the bird in a large roasting tin in the middle of the oven. Roast for the calculated time according to size (page 134–5) except that the oven temperature must be raised to 230°C (450°F) Gas 8 and the coverings removed for the last 30 minutes to crisp the skin. Turn off the oven but leave the turkey in the oven. If you don't have a second oven, leave it on, remove the turkey from the oven, cover with a tent of foil and leave in a warm place.

Spoon some of the turkey fat from the roasting tin into a second tin, add the potatoes, turn to coat with the fat and roast for about 1 hour. Cook the chipolatas and bacon rolls.

Using oven gloves, or rubber gloves specially reserved for the occasion, tip out any free juices from the cavity, then lift the turkey onto the serving platter. Return it to the oven, leaving the door open until the temperature has dropped and will no longer cook the bird. Pour off the gravy juices, preferably into a gravy separator or jug to lift off the fat. Reheat with the seasoned stock. Use to fill a gravy boat, reserving the rest in a Thermos for second helpings. Serve with bacon rolls, chipolatas, sausage meat patties, bread sauce, Brussels sprouts and roast potatoes.

**Stuffed turkey meat is often dry. If you add a juicy filling and buttery herb gravy, it will be transformed into a deliciously moist, light, lunch dish. Serve with baby new potatoes and Glazed Roast Carrots (page 27) for special occasions.**

# rolled turkey breast
## with spinach, bacon and cheese

a small boneless breast of turkey, about 550 g

250 g cooked chopped spinach

freshly grated nutmeg

4 slices of back bacon

250 g Cheddar or Gruyère cheese, thinly sliced

2 tablespoons olive or sunflower oil

sea salt and freshly ground black pepper

**herb gravy**

300 ml strong chicken stock

175 g unsalted butter

1 tablespoon chopped fresh flat leaf parsley

2 teaspoons chopped fresh tarragon

*kitchen string*
*an instant-read thermometer*

**serves 4**

Put the turkey breast skin side down on a flat board and hit it 2–3 times with the side of a heavy cleaver or meat mallet to flatten it. Cut a horizontal slice off the thickest part of the breast to even it up more, and use it to cover a thinner part. Season the turkey with salt and pepper and season the spinach with plenty of nutmeg.

Overlap the bacon slices to cover the inside surface of the meat and cover this with the spinach. Make a third layer with slices of cheese. Roll up the turkey into a roll and tie it neatly with kitchen string. Brush it all over with the oil. Roast in the middle of a preheated oven at 200°C (400°F) Gas 6 for 1 hour or until an instant-read thermometer measures 82°C (180°F). Baste the turkey frequently with some of the stock for the herb gravy.

When the turkey is done, remove from the oven and transfer to a serving dish. Remove and discard the string. Reserve any roasting juices and any more that collect in the serving dish.

To make the gravy, put the butter, remaining stock, parsley and tarragon in a saucepan and bring to the boil. Add the juices from the roasting tin and the serving dish.

Slice the turkey crossways and serve with the herb gravy.

**Many Scandinavians celebrate Christmas on Christmas Eve, often with roast goose or duck, while in Britain our big celebratory meal is lunch on Christmas Day. The traditional accompaniments for this bird are the apples and prunes used to stuff the goose, plus red cabbage cooked with a tart berry juice such as blackcurrant, plus sugar-glazed potatoes. The combination of rich meat, fruit, plus tart and sweet vegetables is common in many cuisines.**

# scandinavian roast goose

1 goose, about 6 kg

250 g pitted prunes

500 g tart apples,
peeled, cored and quartered

75 ml red wine

1 tablespoon cornflour,
mixed with 1 tablespoon water

150–300 ml chicken stock

3–4 tablespoons cream

sea salt and freshly ground black pepper

**to serve**

boiled potatoes browned in sugar

sweet pickles

Danish Red Cabbage (page 122)

*an instant-read thermometer*

**serves 6**

Dry the goose inside and out with kitchen paper, then rub with salt and pepper and prick the skin all over with a skewer or sharp-pronged fork.

Scald the prunes with boiling water and stuff the goose with the apples and prunes. Rub the skin with salt.

Put the goose breast up on a rack in a roasting tin. Put in a cold oven, turn to 170°C (325°F) Gas 3 and roast for 45 minutes. Add a little cold water to the pan and roast for 3½ hours or according to size (see chart page 133). Take care not to let the water dry up – add extra as necessary. The goose is done when an instant-read thermometer reaches 82°C (180°F). Alternatively, the juices should run clear when you prick the leg at the thickest part. Waggle the leg bone a little – it should move in the socket. Transfer the bird to a platter.

Lift all but 2 tablespoons of fat from the tin into a gravy separator. Pour the gravy juices into a small bowl and stir in the cornflour mixture (keep the goose fat for another use). Increase the oven temperature to 250°C (500°F) Gas 9. Return the goose to the roasting tin, pour 2 tablespoons cold water over the breast and return the bird to the oven.

Pour the wine into a clean saucepan, add 1 tablespoon of the goose fat, bring to the boil and reduce until syrupy. Add the gravy juices mixture and the stock and return to the boil, stirring all the time. Season well with salt and pepper and stir in the cream.

Carve the goose and serve with the gravy, boiled potatoes browned in caramel sugar, sweet pickles and Danish red cabbage.

You can buy pheasant breasts separately in butcher's shops and supermarkets, and this is a delicious way to prepare them. If you have the legs as well, use them to make a stock. Otherwise, use good quality chicken stock available in tubs or cartons.

# boned, rolled and stuffed pheasant breasts with whisky

4 boneless pheasant breasts

50 g unsalted butter

3 tablespoons whisky

300 ml chicken or pheasant stock

1 tablespoon cornflour

sea salt and freshly ground black pepper

**whisky stuffing**

50 g onions, chopped

50 g sultanas

50 g dates, pitted, washed, dried and chopped

60 g unsalted butter,
plus 2 tablespoons extra, for basting

6 tablespoons whisky

1½ tablespoons cider vinegar

**to serve**

sautéed potatoes

Roast Apples and Celeriac (page 26)

Cranberry Relish (page 120)

*a piping bag (optional)*

*cocktail sticks*

*an instant-read thermometer*

**serves 4**

To make the stuffing, remove the fillets from the pheasant breasts and chop them into small pieces, discarding any sinew. Put the onions, sultanas, dates, butter and whisky in a saucepan, bring to the boil, reduce the heat and cook gently until all the liquid has been absorbed. Add the chopped fillets, stir in the vinegar and bring to the boil to cook the fillets. Season with salt and pepper, cool and spoon the stuffing into a piping bag, if using.

Rub the breasts with 25 g of the butter, salt and pepper, roll them into a loose cylinder and secure with a cocktail stick. Holding them in the palm of your hand, pipe the stuffing into the centres or fill them with a spoon. Turn them over so they are skin side up. Set them, side by side, in a roasting tin and roast in a preheated oven at 250°C (500°F) Gas 9 for 20 minutes until just firm, or when an instant-read thermometer registers 82°C (180°F). Remove from the oven and transfer to a serving dish.

Heat the roasting tin on top of the stove, add the whisky and stir and scrape up all the delicious sediment. Bring to the boil, then simmer for a few minutes to drive off the alcohol. Add the stock, remaining butter and cornflour to the tin, stir well, bring to the boil and let bubble for a couple of minutes to thicken it. Pour the juices around the pheasant breasts. Serve on a bed of sautéed potatoes with the roasted apples and celeriac and cranberry relish.

Foxes love the flavour of guinea fowl (or 'gleanies' as they are called in Cornwall), so if you wanted one for supper, you waited till nightfall, climbed a tree and lifted off the bird of your choice, because that's where you'd find them hiding from their predators. Now farming has made guinea fowl life so much less dangerous and they're all reared in enclosures. Tiny, dark Puy lentils originate from Le Puy in France and are a favourite with cooks. If unavailable, use other brown lentils.

# guinea fowl with puy lentils

2 guinea fowl

2 tablespoons brandy or Calvados

500 ml chicken stock

2 teaspoons chopped fresh tarragon

12 chipolata sausages,
preferably made with venison

1 teaspoon cornflour, mixed with
1 tablespoon water

sea salt

**bed of vegetables**

2 tablespoons olive oil or melted butter

6 small onions, peeled

3 carrots, diced

150 g or 6 slices of back bacon

**lentils**

175 g Puy lentils, rinsed and drained

½ teaspoon dried thyme
or 2 sprigs fresh, chopped

1 bay leaf

a pinch of salt

*an instant-read thermometer*

**serves 6**

Rinse the lentils well, put in a saucepan, add the thyme, bay leaf and a little salt, then cover them with 1 litre water. Cook until soft and the water has been absorbed, adding more water during the cooking if they dry out before becoming tender.

To prepare the bed of vegetables, heat the oil in a roasting tin on top of the stove, add the onions, carrots and bacon, fry until browned and remove to a plate. Add the birds to the tin and brown them on all sides, sprinkling them with a little salt. Pour the brandy over them. Stand back and ignite it. When the flames have gone out, return the vegetables and bacon to the pan and tuck them around the guinea fowl. Add the stock and half the tarragon, then roast in a preheated oven at 170°C (325°F) Gas 3 for 1½ hours or until an instant-read thermometer registers 80°C (175°F). Put the chipolatas in the tin for the last 20 minutes of cooking time.

Lift the guinea fowl and chipolatas onto a platter and cut the birds into 6 portions each. Keep them warm. Add the cornflour to the pan and stir it through the vegetables and stock. Bring to the boil, add the lentils and the rest of the tarragon and ladle onto a serving dish or 6 heated dinner plates. Arrange the guinea fowl on top and serve with the chipolata sausages.

Venison is an umbrella word covering the meat of many kinds of deer. The saddle of these animals, wild or farmed, is almost always tender, and so is the haunch when taken from a young one, but it is still a good idea to tenderize the meat further by hanging it for a while. A good butcher will often do this for you. Adding wine and spices, especially pepper, not only adds flavour, but in the past helped to keep the meat in good condition.

# marinated roast venison

Open the saddle and cut away all the loose trimmings from around the rib area and any excess flank, leaving enough to wrap around the meat. To make a stock, put the trimmings, onion, red wine and 500 ml water in a saucepan. Bring to the boil, reduce the heat and simmer gently for 1 hour.

To make the marinade, put the butter or oil, juniper berries, thyme, garlic, anchovies, salt and pepper in a bowl and mix well. Rub the opened saddle with half the marinade and sprinkle with the port, arrange the pork fat or bacon lengthways along the backbone cavity, top with the sprigs of rosemary, close the meat up and tie it with string. Rub the outside with the rest of the marinade, wrap the meat in foil or greaseproof paper and leave in a cool place for at least 3 hours.

Unwrap the meat and put it in a preheated oven at 250°C (450°F) Gas 7 for 10 minutes, then reduce to 170°C (325°F) Gas 3 for 45 minutes or until an instant-read thermometer registers 65°C (150°F). Baste the meat with the pan juices 2–3 times during this period. Transfer the meat to a serving dish and keep it warm, discarding the string. The temperature will continue to rise to 70°C (160°F).

To make the gravy, put the roasting tin on the top of the stove. Add the redcurrant jelly and stock and let it boil until the jelly dissolves, then add the cornflour mixture, return to the boil, season with salt and pepper and add any juices collected from the roast. Serve the gravy in a jug.

Carve the meat straight across the grain, not lengthways as is often done with a saddle. Serve with sweet potatoes, fennel and pan-fried brown button mushrooms.

1 venison saddle, about 2 kg, boned and rolled

**stock**

½ onion, chopped

250 ml red wine

**marinade**

60 g softened butter or 4 tablespoons olive oil

12 juniper berries, crushed

½ teaspoon dried thyme

2 garlic cloves, crushed

5 salted anchovies, well rinsed, then chopped

1 tablespoon port

a strip of pork fat or 3 slices streaky bacon, made into long rolls

3 sprigs of rosemary

sea salt and freshly ground black pepper

**gravy**

1 tablespoon redcurrant jelly

1 tablespoon cornflour, mixed with 125 ml water

**to serve**

Sweet Potatoes en Brochette (page 20)

Fennel Roasted in Butter (page 15)

pan-fried brown button mushrooms

*kitchen string*

*kitchen foil or greaseproof paper*

*an instant-read thermometer*

**serves 8–10**

**A rabbit has to be young if it is to be roasted. Only the very young ones should be roasted whole, giving the most tender pure white meat imaginable. Otherwise it is best to cut the meat into pieces, frying the legs in butter first to give them a bit of colour, then roasting them with the saddle. Some supermarkets sell prepared rabbit pieces – you will need about 1 kg. Rosemary and thyme are the traditional herb flavourings, while cider gives a little bit of pungency to the gravy.**

# roast rabbit with herbs and cider

4 wild rabbits, about 500 g each or 2 farmed ones

1 onion, chopped

1 carrot, sliced

1 bay leaf

12 slices streaky bacon

100 g butter

3 tip sprigs of rosemary, or 1 long one, broken into 3, or 1 teaspoon dried rosemary

6–8 tip sprigs of thyme, 2–3 whole sprigs or ½ teaspoon dried thyme

200 ml cider

2 tablespoons double cream (optional)

sea salt and freshly ground black pepper

*an instant-read thermometer*

**serves 4**

First cut the legs and saddle off each rabbit and reserve with the kidneys. To make a stock, put the bones in a saucepan, add the onion, carrot and bay leaf, cover with water and simmer for about 1 hour. Strain off and reserve the stock, discard the bones, and reserve the onion and carrot*.

Loosen the tough membrane around the saddles by sliding the point of a sharp knife along the backbone from under the neck end to the tail, freeing the meat underneath. Do one side at a time, then cut off and discard it. Cover the saddle with strips of bacon.

Melt the butter in a frying pan, add the legs and fry for about 5 minutes to give them a bit of colour. Season with salt, pepper, rosemary and thyme. Put the reserved onion and carrot in a roasting tin and set the legs and saddle on top. Roast in the middle of a preheated oven at 230°C (450°F) Gas 8 for 15–20 minutes according to size or until an instant-read thermometer registers 70°C (160°F).

Meanwhile, add the kidneys to the pan used to brown the legs, adding a little extra butter if necessary. Fry gently until firm, then remove and set aside until serving time. Deglaze the pan with the cider, add the stock and the cream, if using, and reduce the gravy to increase the flavour and thicken it. Add salt and pepper to taste.

Arrange the meat and kidneys on a serving dish and pour the sauce over the top.

* If you have used ready-prepared rabbit pieces, feel free to use fresh chicken stock, either homemade or from the supermarket, instead.

meat

# roast beef with all the trimmings

Only the very best meat should be used for this delicious roast, and you are in the hands of your butcher for that, so choose him well! The art is not so much in the cooking as in the timing, so you don't end up with everybody waiting for you at the table, while you have forgotten to make the gravy or put the Yorkshire pudding in early enough. Oven timings have to be worked out, even though the guesswork is taken out when an instant-read thermometer is used. This routine works for me and I hope you can use it too. This timetable, for serving a roast at 1:00 pm, assumes 3 kg beef on the bone, which will take about 1 hour 40 minutes plus 20 minutes resting time – 2 hours in all.

3 kg bone-in forerib of beef (2–3 bones)

2 tablespoons plain flour

1 tablespoon hot mustard powder

75 g beef dripping, shortening or 4 tablespoons olive oil

3 onions, quartered

8–10 potatoes, cut into chunks and par-boiled

5–6 parsnips, halved lengthways

sea salt and freshly ground black pepper

**accompaniments**

1 recipe Horseradish Sauce (page 124)

1 recipe Yorkshire Puddings (page 124)

1.25 kg green vegetable, such as cabbage, sliced and steamed or boiled

1 recipe Gravy (page 120)

*an instant-read thermometer*

**serves 8–10**

**10:45**  Oven on to 240°C (475°F) Gas 8. Season the meat, mix the flour and the mustard and pat it onto the beef fat. Put the dripping or oil in the roasting tin, put the onions in the middle and set the beef, fat side up, on top.

**11:00**  Put the potatoes and parsnips around the meat and put the tin in the oven.

**11:10**  Make the horseradish sauce and set aside.

**11:20**  Reduce oven heat to 190°C (375°F) Gas 5, baste the beef and turn the vegetables in the fat.

**11:40**  Baste the beef and turn the potatoes and parsnips in the fat.

**12:10**  Repeat.

**12:29**  Increase the oven temperature to 240°C (475°F) Gas 8 and spoon 4 tablespoons of the fat into the large Yorkshire pudding tin, if using.

**12:30**  Heat the fat on the top of the stove and pour the Yorkshire pudding batter into the tin, or wait to do this until 12:42 if you are making individual Yorkshire puddings (see below).

**12:31**  Put the Yorkshire pudding tin in the oven.

**12:33**  Put the green vegetable on to boil. Insert a meat thermometer into the beef.

**12:40**  Take the beef out now, or when thermometer registers 60°C (175°F) (or a little below if you like beef very rare). Lift the beef onto a serving dish, add the vegetables and set aside in a warm place. It will go on cooking as it rests.

**12:42**  Spoon off the fat and retain it for another time, or spoon into the small Yorkshire pudding tins, pour in the batter, then put in the oven.

**12:45**  Make the gravy in the roasting tin and pour into a gravy boat.

**12:50**  Dish up the green vegetables and keep them warm.

**12:58**  Serve the Yorkshire pudding around the beef or on a separate platter.

**1:00**  Put the beef on the table with the horseradish sauce and the gravy.

**To many connoisseurs, this is the cut that gives the true, full flavour of beef. No nonsense about having it rare or medium or whatever – this is always well done (and slowly), but it is still a roast. The piece of meat nearest the bone (or where it used to be, because the brisket is boneless) is the tenderest piece, but as always it is the quality of the meat that tells. The meat may be cooked for even longer at the low temperature without any loss of flavour or texture, and some people say the longer the better. Keep basting and stirring.**

# slow-roasted brisket
## and vegetables

1.5 kg beef brisket, boned but not rolled

4 onions, cut into chunks

4 carrots, cut into chunks

4 celery stalks, cut into 5 cm slices

your choice of other vegetables, such as parsnips, leeks and celeriac

4 medium potatoes, par-boiled and quartered

sea salt and freshly ground black pepper

**serves 4–6**

Season the meat with salt and pepper and put in a large roasting tin.

Put the tin in a cold oven and turn the temperature to 250°C (500°F) Gas 9 for the first 40 minutes. This will start the fat running. Add the onions, carrots, celery and your choice of other vegetables – but not the potatoes. Stir them around to coat with the fat and season lightly with salt and pepper. Reduce the oven temperature to 170°C (325°F) Gas 3.

After another 40 minutes, pour in 500 ml hot water, baste the meat and stir the vegetables with a wooden spoon. Repeat after a further 40 minutes, judging the quantity of water to be added. There should be enough for basting, but the meat should not be awash with liquid. Add the potatoes.

Baste again after another 40 minutes, this time without adding water, and then increase the temperature to 220°C (425°F) Gas 7 for the last 20 minutes.

Remove the roasting tin from the oven and transfer the meat to a large plate. Keep it warm. Pour off all the liquid from the roasting tin into a gravy separator and then into a jug, leaving most of the fat behind.

Dish up the meat onto a large serving platter with the vegetables around it. Serve the jug of gravy separately.

This cut is the most tender of all and easy to cook – you just roast it to the pinkness you require. However, this can be a bit dull, so some salty, smoky ham and sweet port and mushrooms will give it all the extra flavour it needs. Cooked to this recipe, then let rest, the meat will be a gentle rosy pink all through when it is carved. An added bonus is that it is also delicious served cold with a salad and chutney next day.

# fillet of beef and mushrooms
## wrapped in parma ham

30 g unsalted butter

1 small onion, chopped

150 g mushrooms, sliced

2 tablespoons port mixed with 1 tablespoon brandy

12 slices Parma ham

750 g fillet of beef

sea salt and freshly ground black pepper

**to serve**

fresh Horseradish Sauce (page 124)

sautéed potatoes

steamed runner beans

*an instant-read thermometer*

**serves 4–6**

Melt the butter in a frying pan, add the onion and cook gently for 5 minutes until softened. Add the mushrooms and cook until they have absorbed all the butter and become softened too, adding more butter if necessary.

Season with salt and pepper, then remove the pan from the heat to add the port and brandy mixture, letting it sizzle and lose the alcohol before returning it to the stove. Reduce the liquid until it has all been absorbed by the mushrooms. Cool and set aside.

Arrange 6 slices of ham crossways on a roasting tray, overlapping them to fit the length of the meat. Spread the mushroom mixture over the ham to cover it, then season the beef and set it on top. Cover with the remaining ham, tucking the slices under and around so that no beef is visible.

Roast in a preheated oven at 220°C (425°F) Gas 7 for 40 minutes or until an instant-read thermometer registers 60°C (140°F). Turn off the oven and leave the door open. The internal temperature of the meat will continue to rise to 70°C (158°F), when it will be an even rosy pink when sliced. Serve with fresh horseradish sauce, sautéed potatoes and steamed runner beans.

**Note** The usual timings given for other cuts of beef do not apply to fillets. This is because they are long and thin, and the heat only need get through this narrow thickness. The timing will be the same, no matter how long the fillet is.

**This cut of beef is often prepared by a butcher ready to be sliced into steaks, but it can be bought in a whole piece and is the easiest cut to carve. The meat is very tender and except, for the outside, is free from fat.**

# roast boned beef loin
## basted with wine gravy

1.5 kg strip loin of beef
(boned sirloin, without the undercut)

3 garlic cloves, sliced

6 small tip sprigs of thyme

100 g unsalted butter

2 onions, sliced

125 ml red wine

sea salt and coarsely ground black pepper

*an instant-read thermometer*

**serves 6**

Trim off a sheet of fat from the top of the meat and keep it to use as a cushion under the roast. Make 6 slits in the underside of the meat and push in a sliver of garlic and a sprig of thyme. Season with the salt and pepper and spread half the butter generously over the underside of the meat. Set the fat in the roasting pan and put the sliced onions on top. Add the sirloin and roast in a preheated oven at 220°C (425°F) Gas 7 for 20 minutes.

Pour the wine into the pan, let it bubble for a moment, then spoon it over the beef. Continue to cook the meat until it is done to your liking, preferably pink, or when an instant-read thermometer registers 65°C (150°F). Base the meat frequently, adding water to the pan when the wine becomes low.

Transfer the meat to a carving platter and let rest it in a warm place for 10 minutes.

To make a light gravy, add 25 ml water to the roasting tin and stir it through the reduced wine. Stir in the remaining butter to make a sauce. Strain into a saucepan, bring to the boil, then add salt and pepper to taste. Serve in a separate sauceboat.

---

**The hand test**

A chef's trick for testing for doneness is to compare the texture to your hand.
• Keep your hand flat with the thumb and fingers closed. Pinch the thumb mound – the texture equals rare.
• Open the thumb wide and pinch the thumb mound – the texture equals medium.
• Spread the fingers and thumb wide and pinch the thumb mound – the texture equals well done (something all chefs would prefer to avoid).

**The pinch test**

If you don't have
an instant-read meat
thermometer, a
time-honoured way of
testing for doneness is
to pinch a lean surface.
If it springs back easily,
it is rare; if less
springy, it is medium;
if firm, it is well done.

This delicious fat-free cut of beef is not the tenderest piece for roasting, but it has a great deal of flavour. Cook it slowly for most of the time, then turn the heat up at the end to give it a good roasting flavour. The meat is cut in two places to make pockets for the stuffing. This recipe is based on an old Italian original, and similar dishes are found in Central Europe. It produces both rare and medium meat, so all tastes can be catered for.

# roast stuffed topside
## with mustard and green peppercorns

1.5 kg beef topside

sea salt and freshly ground black pepper

**stuffing**

60 g cream cheese

1 teaspoon Dijon mustard

1 teaspoon green peppercorns preserved in brine, or coarsely ground black pepper

6 Swiss chard leaves

**gravy**

1 teaspoon plain flour

250 ml beef stock

*kitchen string*

*an instant-read thermometer*

**serves 4**

Cut a the meat one-third of the way through its thickness, leaving it attached on one side. Turn the meat over and make another cut one-third of the way down, again leaving it attached on one side, producing 3 thick layers of meat in a Z-shape. Using a sharp knife, carefully remove any gristle that you come across. Season the meat well.

To make the stuffing, put the cream cheese, mustard and peppercorns in a bowl and mash with a fork. Spread the mixture evenly between the layers, adding chard leaves to each layer. Tie up the meat with string to keep the stuffing inside.

Put the meat in a roasting tin and cook in a preheated oven at 250°C (500°F) Gas 9 for 10 minutes. Reduce the temperature to 180°C (350°F) Gas 4 and continue cooking until an instant-read thermometer registers 50°C (120°F) internal temperature.

Finally, increase the temperature to 250°C (500°F) Gas 9 again to crisp up the surface, and when the thermometer registers 65°C (150°F), remove the meat from the oven and transfer to a serving platter. Let rest for 15–20 minutes.

To make the gravy, pour off all but 1 tablespoon of fat from the roasting tin and put over medium heat on top of the stove. Add the flour and stir into the fat to make a roux. Pour in the stock and bring to the boil, whisking constantly.

Carve the meat thickly, then serve with the gravy in a sauceboat.

**A quick and simple way to entertain is to blast a boned piece of tender rib in the oven. Top-quality meat from a small steer is a vital factor in the success of this dish. Gristle or loose texture from a lesser-quality animal would make it tougher and more difficult to carve.**

# french-carved rib steak

single first rib of the sirloin, boned

sea salt flakes

**seasoning**

2 tablespoons olive oil

2 garlic cloves, crushed

2 teaspoons Dijon mustard

sea salt and coarsely ground black pepper

**to serve cold (optional)**

crusty bread

rocket leaves

fresh Horseradish Sauce (page 124)

*roasting tin with a rack*

**serves 2**

To make the seasoning mixture, put the olive oil, garlic, mustard, salt and pepper in a bowl and mix well. Spread half the seasoning on the upper side of the meat. Put the meat on a rack in a roasting tin and cook in a preheated oven at 250°C (500°F) Gas 9 or maximum for 5 minutes.

Turn the meat over, spread with the rest of the seasoning and cook for a further 5 minutes or less, according to the required state of 'doneness'. Crunch over some sea salt before serving, carved in thick diagonal slices.

You can also serve this cold next day, with crusty bread, rocket and horseradish.

**Roasting a breast of veal is similar to cooking a piece of beef brisket, but the taste is very different and it takes less time. The preliminary browning is done over high heat on top of the stove, then the meat is transferred to the oven for gentle roasting. Wine, garlic and rosemary turn this into a classic Italian favourite.**

# slow-roasted breast of veal

60 g unsalted butter

2 tablespoons olive oil

2 onions, cut into chunks

6 celery stalks, cut into 2 cm lengths

1.5 kg breast of veal, on the bone

2–3 sprigs of rosemary

200 ml white wine

3 garlic cloves, crushed with a knife

1 teaspoon tomato paste

sea salt and freshly ground black pepper

**serves 4**

Put the butter and oil in a heavy frying pan and set over high heat. When the butter begins to colour, add the onions and celery, turn them over in the fat and fry them until they colour a little. Lower the heat so the butter doesn't burn. This will take about 10 minutes. Spoon them into a roasting tin.

Put the seasoned meat bone side up in the frying pan and brown it well. Turn it over, add the rosemary and brown the underside lightly.

Lift the meat into the roasting tin and transfer to a preheated oven at 170°C (325°F) Gas 3. Add the wine, garlic and tomato paste to the frying pan. Bring to the boil, then simmer the liquid until it is reduced and syrupy. Add 200 ml water, bring to the boil, then pour it and all the bits in the pan into the roasting tin. Roast the meat, basting it from time to time until tender, usually about 2 hours. You may need to top up with water from time to time to keep the vegetables moist.

Lift the veal onto a carving platter and either cut the meat into thick slices between the bones or, using a sharp knife, remove the bones, which should slide out quite easily. You can then carve the meat into thinner slices. Serve the vegetables with the meat.

The delicate flavour of veal with cream or cheese is a popular combination everywhere from Italy to Denmark. This recipe has a similarly international pedigree. It was given to a friend in Melbourne by a Polish poet who grew up in Russia before migrating to Australia. Sour cream is different in different countries. In Eastern and Central Europe – and Australia – it is thick and delicious, a little like mascarpone, and can be used straight on the veal. It reduces to become a dill-flavoured cheese coating on the meat. In other parts of the world, the cream needs some extra preparation. Serve this rich and delicate dish with a peppery watercress salad (and potatoes of course).

# **veal** with mustard cream

1.5 kg piece of veal (cushion or topside)

2 tablespoons melted butter or olive oil

sea salt and freshly ground black pepper

**sour cream crust**

75 ml sour cream

75 ml double cream,
plus 2 tablespoons extra
for the gravy (optional)

1 teaspoon Dijon mustard

1 tablespoon lemon juice

2 tablespoons chopped fresh dill

*kitchen foil*

*an instant-read thermometer*

**serves 6**

Put the sour cream, double cream, mustard and 1 teaspoon of the lemon juice in a bowl and mix well.

Season the meat well with salt and pepper and brush it all over with the melted butter or oil. Set the meat on a sheet of kitchen foil and coat it with the dill, patting it on to make it cling.

Smother the meat with the sour cream mixture and pull up the edges of the foil to partly cover the meat, leaving the top exposed. Pour in any remaining melted butter and the remaining lemon juice. Put the parcel in a roasting tin, and transfer to a preheated oven at 170°C (325°F) Gas 3. After about 1 hour, lift out the tin and open the foil to expose the juices that have collected at the bottom. Baste the meat with the juices (but avoid the crust which is forming on the top) and add 1 tablespoon water to the juices if there are not enough to moisten the meat.

Return the meat to the oven for a further 30 minutes and if the crust has not browned, raise the oven temperature to 200°C (400°F) Gas 6 for 15 minutes, or until an instant-read thermometer registers 71°C (160°F).

Lift the veal onto a large platter and drain the juices from the roasting tin into a saucepan. Add the 2 tablespoons cream, reheat gently and serve separately for guests to help themselves.

There are so many flavours that can be introduced to the classic leg of lamb and each country has its favourites. Britain likes it just plain with mint sauce, Australians, New Zealanders and French stick it with slivers of garlic and sprigs of rosemary, while Italians love the combined flavour of lemon and garlic, with the salty seasoning in the gravy supplied by anchovies. Be adventurous – ask the butcher to tunnel-bone a more mature lamb and season the centre with crushed juniper berries.

# italian roast leg of lamb
## with lemon and anchovy sauce

1 leg of lamb, 2.5–3 kg

2 garlic cloves, thinly sliced

1 tablespoon olive oil

175 ml white wine

sea salt and freshly ground black pepper

**sauce**

5 anchovy fillets

175 ml chicken stock

grated lemon zest from 1 unwaxed lemon

1 tablespoon chopped fresh flat leaf parsley

*an instant-read thermometer*

**serves 5**

Make slits in the meat in several places and insert the slivers of garlic. Brush the lamb with the oil and season with salt and pepper. Set it in a roasting tin and pour the wine around. Roast in a preheated oven at 200°C (400°F) Gas 6 until an instant-read thermometer registers 63°C (145°F) for medium rare or cook at 170°C (325°F) Gas 3 for well done meat until the thermometer registers 77°C (170°F). This takes 1¼–1½ hours. Baste the meat from time to time, adding water if the wine becomes low.

When the lamb is cooked to your liking, transfer it to a serving dish and let rest in a warm place while you make the gravy. Discard any excess fat from the roasting tin, then add the anchovies, crushing them to a paste with a fork. Stir in the stock until the anchovies have been absorbed. Add the lemon zest and parsley and any juices that have come out of the lamb during the resting period, then pour into a sauceboat to serve.

The lower part of the lamb leg was always the cook's perk in our house. It was carved off the leg for my mother, who thought it was the best part, with all the delicious melting gelatinous threads running through. Nowadays, we don't have to wait for someone to cook a leg, because the shanks are sold separately. They are much more tender than the equivalent shin of beef.

# slow-roasted lamb shanks
## with chillies

4 lamb shanks

2 tablespoons olive oil

**tex-mex spices***

½ teaspoon garlic powder

½ teaspoon ground red chilli

½ teaspoon dried oregano

½ teaspoon chilli flakes

1 teaspoon salt

½ teaspoon coarsely ground black pepper

Roast Potatoes (page 16), to serve

**sauce**

1 tablespoon olive oil

2 garlic cloves, crushed

2 teaspoons hot oak-smoked paprika

1 teaspoon ground cumin

1 tablespoon red wine vinegar

6 beef or large tomatoes, skinned, halved and deseeded

2 tablespoons chopped fresh mint

½ teaspoon sugar

sea salt and freshly ground black pepper

**red kidney beans**

400 g cooked or canned red kidney beans

1 tablespoon olive oil

sea salt and freshly ground black pepper

**serves 4**

Brush the shanks with the olive oil. Put the garlic powder, ground red chilli, oregano, chilli flakes, salt and pepper in a bowl, mix well, then sprinkle over the shanks.

Set the shanks end to end in a roasting tin. Put in the middle of a preheated oven and cook at at 150°C (300°F) Gas 2 for 2 hours, turning them over 2–3 times. Remove from the oven and let rest for 30 minutes.

To make the sauce, heat the oil in a large pan, add the garlic and cook to a light brown (it will give off a delicious roasting aroma). Add the paprika and cumin and cook for 1 minute without letting them burn. Pour in the vinegar, then add the tomatoes, breaking them up with a wooden spoon and cooking to form a lumpy sauce. Add the mint, season with salt and pepper and add sugar to taste.

To prepare the red kidney beans, drain and transfer to a small saucepan, stir in the olive oil, add salt and pepper to taste, then heat gently.

Dish up the shanks, pour off any excess fat and add 2–3 tablespoons water to the tin to make a little stock. Stir well, then add it to the sauce. Bring to the boil, then season with salt and pepper and add more sugar if necessary. Pour the sauce over the meat and serve with roast potatoes and red kidney beans.

* Many supermarkets sell ready-made Tex-Mex spice mixes. Use 1½ tablespoons and mix with the salt.

This is the perfect way to cook lamb chops if you don't know exactly when you are going to have to dish them up, because they can wait for up to 2 hours before finishing them. To French-trim two 6-or 7-rib racks for 4 people, ask the butcher to cut away each backbone where it joins the ribs – this is called 'chining'. Now that the ribs are free, you can cut the racks in half between the middle ribs and discard the end rib on the half that has 4 (or keep them for a cook's treat later). Shorten the ribs to about 3–4 cm beyond the meat, then cut out the meat between each rib and scrape the bones clean. All these trimmings can be used to make stock.

# rack of lamb
## with redcurrant sauce

2 racks of lamb, French-trimmed (see recipe introduction)

about 500 g baby spinach, wilted

### marinating syrup

2 tablespoons redcurrant jelly

125 ml sweet sherry

125 ml sherry vinegar

3 tablespoons sugar

2 tablespoons soy sauce

2 sprigs of rosemary

2 small garlic cloves, sliced

### gravy

25 g unsalted butter

125 ml white vermouth

250 ml lamb or chicken stock

sea salt and freshly ground black pepper

*non-stick baking parchment or kitchen foil*

**serves 4–6**

To make the marinating syrup, put the redcurrant jelly in a saucepan, add the sherry, vinegar, sugar, soy sauce, rosemary and 3 slices of the garlic and boil to reduce and form a syrup. Brush the syrup all over the racks of lamb and put them in a plastic bag, with the rest of the syrup and set aside to marinate for 2 hours, turning them every 30 minutes.

When ready to cook, wipe the excess marinade off the racks of lamb, set them on non-stick parchment or a sheet of kitchen foil in a roasting tin and roast in a preheated oven at 250°C (500°F) Gas 9 for 8 minutes. Remove from the oven and let rest in a warm place for up to 2 hours.

To serve, reheat the racks for 6–8 minutes in the very hot oven, then slice them between the bones. Put a bed of cooked spinach on each plate, then put the cutlets on top, crossing over the bones.

Meanwhile, to make the gravy, put the butter in a small saucepan, add the vermouth and boil until reduced by half. Add the stock and 2–3 teaspoons of the marinade, bring to the boil and reduce again to improve the flavour. Season to taste with salt and pepper, pour around the meat, then serve.

This dish is for Christmas time – the spices lightly pickle the meat and give it an intriguing Eastern flavour. They must be rubbed in dry so the flavours penetrate the meat, then later the oil is added to moisten it. Because there is a great deal of fatless meat on a ham, it will dry out and toughen unless basted frequently. If you are using the trotter end of a half leg, wrap it with a thick collar of foil during the later part of the cooking to keep it moist. The meat taken from the top end of the leg may be tunnel-boned for easier carving. It is delicious cold.

# spiced roast ham or pork
## with juniper berries

½ leg of pork or gammon, about 2.5 kg

2–3 tablespoons peanut or sunflower oil

275 ml water or chicken stock

sea salt

**spice mixture**

1 teaspoon ground coriander

1 teaspoon ground cumin

1 teaspoon ground caraway

1 teaspoon ground ginger

½ teaspoon ground cinnamon

½ teaspoon ground allspice

½ teaspoon freshly grated nutmeg

12 juniper berries, crushed

*an instant-read thermometer*

**serves 6**

To prepare the spice mixture, put the coriander, cumin, caraway, ginger, cinnamon, allspice, nutmeg and juniper berries in a bowl and mix well. Remove the rind from the meat and rub the dry spices into all the crevices in the meat. Wrap it in clingfilm or a plastic bag and refrigerate for 48 hours.

Score the fat with a criss cross pattern on the upper side of the meat. Put in a roasting tin, baste with the oil and sprinkle well with salt. Put the tin in the middle of a preheated oven at 240°C (475°F) Gas 8 and add 5–6 tablespoons water. Roast for 10 minutes, then reduce the temperature to 170°C (325°F) Gas 3 and cook for 2½ hours. Baste from time to time and add extra water as necessary to keep it moist because this will form the base of the gravy.

When an instant-read thermometer reaches 80°C (175°F), transfer the meat to a serving dish and let it rest for 10 minutes.

Meanwhile, deglaze the pan with the water or stock to make a gravy, then boil to reduce and intensify the flavours. Taste and, if necessary, adjust the seasoning with salt. Carve the meat in thin slices and serve the gravy separately in a jug.

Without crackling to add texture, pork cries out for some form of flavouring – the loin is the ideal cut for such treatment. Ask your butcher to chine it by removing the backbone, or to cut it down between the ribs, so that you can carve it easily into chops. This is a very dense meat, so gentle roasting is the only way to prevent it drying out, giving ample time for the full flavour to develop.

# slow-roasted pork loin
## with rosemary, madeira and orange

1.5 kg centre loin of pork
200 ml Madeira wine
100 ml freshly squeezed orange juice
2 sprigs of rosemary, bruised
2 oranges, peeled and sliced into 4 slices each
sea salt and freshly ground black pepper

*thick kitchen foil*
*an instant-read thermometer*

**serves 4**

Score the fat with a criss cross pattern and season the meat with plenty of salt and pepper, rubbing it in well. Put a double thickness of kitchen foil in a large roasting tin and turn up the edges. Put in the meat fat side down and pour in the Madeira and juice. Add the rosemary. Leave for about 2 hours if possible, then put in the middle of a preheated oven at 170°C (325°F) Gas 3 and slow-roast for 1 hour.

Carefully turn the meat over, then add the orange slices and about 125 ml water if it is starting to dry out. Cook for a further 30 minutes. Then raise the oven temperature to 220°C (425°F) Gas 7 for a final 10 minutes or until an instant-read thermometer registers 80°C (175°F).

Lift the meat out onto a serving dish and arrange the orange slices around. Carefully pour the juices into a jug, then serve.

This is an ideal cut of pork for serving with crackling: it is tender and moist and will stand the high temperature at the end of the cooking time needed to produce the crunch. Even if you can't get the meat with its outer skin still on, it is still delicious when boned and stuffed with either the traditional sage and onion or a lighter apple and celery filling. If you don't have the rind on the meat, miss out the final high roasting part at the end. Belly of pork works equally well, but it is a lot more fatty and so not to everyone's taste.

2 kg blade or hand of pork, with rind if possible, and scored

1 teaspoon sea salt

2 tablespoons olive oil, for brushing

**stuffing**

1 onion, finely chopped

1 green apple, such as Granny Smith, cut into small pieces

2 celery stalks, finely chopped

60 g cashew nuts, chopped

50 g unsalted butter

2 teaspoons chopped fresh sage leaves

grated zest and freshly squeezed juice of 1 unwaxed lemon

250 g fresh breadcrumbs

**cider gravy**

125 ml cider vinegar

250 ml water or chicken stock

*a roasting tin with a rack*

*a baking tray with sides, or Swiss roll tin*

*an instant-read thermometer*

**serves 6**

# rolled crackly pork roast
## with sage and onion stuffing

To make the stuffing, put the onion, apple, celery, cashews, butter, sage, lemon zest and juice and breadcrumbs in a bowl. Mix well.

Season the inside of the pork with the salt, then spread the stuffing over that side, roll up the meat and tie it with string to make a good shape. Brush with the oil and set it on a rack in a roasting tin. Add 250 ml water. Put it in a cold oven, turn the heat to 220°C (425°F) Gas 7 and roast for 30 minutes.

Reduce the oven temperature to 170°C (325°F) Gas 3. Cook for another 1½ hours or until an instant-read thermometer registers 80°C (175°F). Transfer the meat to another roasting tin or a baking tray with sides. Do not baste during this time.*

Raise the oven temperature to maximum and return the meat to the very hot oven for another 20 minutes to crisp the surface.

Meanwhile, make the gravy by deglazing the roasting tin with the vinegar and reducing it well. Add the water or stock, bring to the boil, then taste and adjust the seasoning with salt if necessary. Serve in a sauceboat.

When the crackling on the meat is ready, transfer the roast to a carving platter and let rest for 10–20 minutes before carving in fairly thick slices.

* I have found that you get better crackling if you don't salt or baste the rind. If the roast doesn't have a rind, then you should baste it 3–4 times during cooking.

**Spareribs make a wonderful supper dish, because they can be cooked in advance and reheated when required. Amazingly, when roasted in the oven, they are more succulent than they are when barbecued (the usual method). Because they are cooked long and slowly, they don't dry out so much.**

# roast sticky spareribs
## marinated and glazed

12 spareribs, about 2 kg

**sticky marinade**

2 tablespoons honey

4 tablespoons soy sauce

1 tablespoon ground ginger

1 tablespoon Dijon mustard

1 tablespoon grated fresh ginger

1 teaspoon oil

**serves 4**

To make the marinade, put the honey, soy sauce, ground ginger, mustard, fresh ginger and oil in a roasting tin and mix well. Add the ribs and turn to coat with the mixture. Set aside for several hours or overnight in the refrigerator.

Remove the tin from the refrigerator about 30 minutes before you want to start cooking, so the ribs can return to room temperature while you preheat the oven.

Roast in a preheated oven at 180°C (350°F) Gas 4 for 1½ hours, turning over after 1 hour. Serve with napkins – this is finger food.

This is every aspiring cook's favourite cut of meat, but unfortunately it is also one that can be overcooked only too easily. This is especially true if the meat is cut into medallions, so cook it as a whole piece, as here, and cut it into medallions later. Serve with mashed potatoes or stir-fried vegetables.

# roast pork fillets
## with creamy thai-spiced sauce

2 pork fillets, 500 g each, trimmed

6 spring onion tops, thickly sliced diagonally

mashed potatoes or stir-fried vegetables, to serve

**vinaigrette marinade**

4 tablespoons rice vinegar

4 tablespoons olive oil

½ teaspoon salt

½ teaspoon Thai seven-spice

**creamy thai-spiced sauce**

3 cm piece fresh ginger, grated

2 tablespoons cider vinegar

4 tablespoons sweet sherry

1 tablespoon peanut or sunflower oil

250 ml coconut milk

1 teaspoon sugar

½ teaspoon Thai seven-spice

a pinch of salt, to taste

*kitchen foil*

**serves 6**

To make a vinaigrette marinade, put the rice vinegar, olive oil, salt and seven-spice in shallow dish, mix well, then add the fillets. Turn to coat with the marinade mixture and set aside for at least 1 hour to marinate.

Put the fillets side by side in a roasting tin, baste them with the marinade and cook in a preheated oven at 250°C (500°F) Gas 9 for 15 minutes, baste again, then roast for a further 15 minutes. Transfer them to a warm place and cover with kitchen foil.

To make the sauce, put the ginger, vinegar, sherry and oil in a small saucepan, heat to simmering and reduce to a syrup. Add the coconut milk, sugar and seven-spice and reduce again to about 125 ml or to taste. Taste and adjust the seasoning.

Just before serving, slice the meat into medallions and pour any juice into the sauce. Serve on heated dinner plates. Spoon the sauce over the top and sprinkle with the spring onions. Serve with mashed potatoes or stir-fried vegetables.

Sometimes this cut is sold without the skin, so it is a good idea to wrap strips of bacon around the meat. The idea is to release some gelatine into the wine to emulsify and combine all the ingredients when you make the gravy. Half a teaspoon of dissolved gelatine added at the end has the same effect, though not the same flavour. Old-fashioned the recipe may be, but it is a classic and still a favourite.

# loin of pork with a herb crust

1.5 kg loin of pork, chined and trimmed

pork rind or 6–7 slices
unsmoked streaky bacon (optional)

2 garlic cloves, 1 cut into slivers, 1 crushed

150 ml red wine

2 tablespoons olive or sunflower oil

60 g fresh breadcrumbs

2 teaspoons chopped fresh thyme

1 tablespoon chopped fresh flat leaf parsley

250 ml beef stock

¼ teaspoon powdered gelatine

2 teaspoons redcurrant jelly

sea salt and freshly ground black pepper

**accompaniments**

mashed potatoes

Fennel Roast in Butter (page 15)

*an instant-read thermometer*

**serves 4**

Remove the rind if it is still on the pork and put the rind skin side down in the roasting pan. Alternatively, use unsmoked streaky bacon or omit altogether. Make several small incisions on the underside of the meat and insert the slivers of garlic (use more if you like). Season the meat with salt and pepper.

Pour the wine into a plastic bag, add 1 tablespoon of the oil, half the thyme, salt, then finally add the meat. Close the bag, excluding as much air as possible and put in a dish in the refrigerator for at least 2 hours.

Preheat the oven to 250°C (500°F) Gas 9, put the meat on top of the rind or bacon in a roasting tin, then lower the heat to 180°C (350°F) Gas 4. Baste with the marinade.

Meanwhile, heat the remaining oil in a pan and add the crushed garlic. When it begins to colour, add the breadcrumbs, the parsley and remaining thyme. Mix to absorb all the oil.

After 1 hour, remove the meat from the oven and pack the seasoned crumbs on top. Don't worry if some fall into the roasting tin – they will act as a gravy thickener later. Baste carefully with the pan juices.

Return the tin to the oven and cook for a further 40 minutes or until an instant-read thermometer registers 80°C (175°F). Lift the meat onto a platter and pour the stock into the pan. Bring to the boil on the top of the stove and, if you're not using pork rind, add the gelatine. Add salt and pepper to taste and melt in the jelly. Serve separately in a jug.

Mashed potatoes are the best thing to mop up the gravy, while roast fennel always goes well with pork (and is a favourite French side dish).

# stuffing, gravy and sauce

# chestnut stuffing
## for turkey or goose

**If you have favourite sausages, such as Toulouse, use them in this stuffing, otherwise ordinary sausage meat is perfectly good. This mixture is much lighter without added breadcrumbs or egg, and is ideal for stuffing the neck of the bird.**

400 g fresh chestnuts (200 g peeled and cooked) or 200 g vacuum-packed chestnuts, ready peeled and cooked

250 ml milk (if using fresh chestnuts)

100 g sausages or sausage meat

2 tablespoons olive oil

1 onion, chopped

150 g turkey liver, chopped (if unavailable, use chicken livers)

60 g streaky bacon, finely chopped

1 tablespoon chopped fresh flat leaf parsley or marjoram (optional)

sea salt and freshly ground black pepper

**makes about 500 g**

If the chestnuts are fresh, they must first be boiled to soften the shell, then peeled while still hot (protect your fingers with rubber gloves).

Put the peeled fresh chestnuts in a saucepan, cover them with the milk and simmer gently until softened, probably 30 minutes but it can take up to 1 hour if they are old ones. Strain them if necessary, weigh out 200 g and put in a bowl.

Crumble the cooked chestnuts with your fingers and use the sausage meat to bind them.

Heat the oil in a frying pan, add the onion, liver and bacon and fry gently until the liver is firm. Stir in the parsley and cook until the mixture begins to brown. Add to the chestnuts with salt and pepper to taste.

**Note** This and other stuffings used in this book may also be cooked separately from the bird. Form into balls and cook in a baking dish at 200°C (400°F) Gas 6 for about 20 minutes.

# apricot stuffing

60 g onions, chopped

60 g cashew nuts

2 celery stalks, coarsely chopped

75 g dried apricots, soaked in 75 ml water

100 g unsalted butter

60 g fresh white breadcrumbs

freshly grated zest of 1 unwaxed orange

freshly squeezed juice of ½ lemon

**makes about 500 g**

Put the onions, cashew nuts, celery and apricots in a food processor. Blend until evenly chopped.

Melt the butter in a saucepan and add the chopped onion mixture. Cook until the nuts begin to brown, then add the crumbs, zest and juice. Transfer to a bowl and let cool. Stuff the bird. If there is any left over, form into cakes and fry in butter in a small frying pan.

# salami stuffing

60 g vacuum-packed chestnuts*

40 g fresh breadcrumbs

100 ml chicken stock

2 tablespoons olive oil

1 garlic clove, crushed

30 g chicken livers

60 g Italian salami, chopped

60 g button mushrooms, chopped

1 teaspoon freshly squeezed lemon juice,
diluted with 1 tablespoon water

2 teaspoons chopped fresh sage

1 egg yolk, beaten

freshly ground black pepper

**enough for a large chicken or small turkey**

Put the chestnuts in a bowl and crumble
them with a fork or between your fingers.
Add the crumbs and stir in the stock.

Put the oil and garlic in a small frying
pan and heat until the garlic begins to
brown. Add the livers and salami, fry for
30 seconds, then add the mushrooms
and diluted lemon juice. Stir well and
cook for another 2 minutes or until
most of the water has evaporated.
Season with plenty of pepper and add
the sage, moist breadcrumbs and
chestnuts. Remove from the heat, let
cool for 5 minutes, then stir in the
beaten egg yolk.

* Pre-roasted, peeled, vacuum-packed
chestnuts are good quality and
convenient. If using fresh chestnuts
prepare as in the recipe on page 117.

# lemon and herb stuffing

**This makes a succulent hot stuffing.
It is also very good when cold and
tastes even better the next day,
when it will have become firm and
easy to slice.**

2 eggs

125 g butter, melted

a handful of fresh parsley leaves

1 teaspoon lemon thyme

freshly grated zest and juice of 1 unwaxed lemon

225 g fresh white breadcrumbs

sea salt and freshly ground black pepper

**enough for a large chicken or small turkey**

Put the eggs, butter, parsley, thyme,
lemon zest and juice in a blender and
work to a smooth purée. Pour it over the
crumbs and mix well. Season to taste
with salt and pepper.

# bread sauce

**A classic with turkey.**

½ onion, finely chopped

½ teaspoon dried thyme

3 whole cloves

500 ml milk

100 g fresh white breadcrumbs

75 g unsalted butter (optional)

2 tablespoons double cream (optional)

sea salt and freshly ground black pepper

**serves 8–10**

Put the onion, thyme, cloves and milk in
a saucepan. Bring gently to the boil over
low heat. Simmer for 5 minutes. Remove
from the heat and set aside for 1 hour.
Remove the cloves.

Add the breadcrumbs, butter and cream,
if using, to the pan. Reheat until nearly
boiling. Stir well, then add salt and
pepper to taste. Set aside for 10 minutes
to thicken, then reheat if necessary
before serving.

# wine gravy

**A classic gravy for any kind of roast – use wine (or brandy) to deglaze the pan, scraping up all the delicious sediments.**

2 tablespoons fat from the pan

4 tablespoons red wine

1 tablespoon plain flour (or more if you like a thicker gravy)

500 ml well-flavoured stock or water

sea salt and freshly ground black pepper

**serves 4–6**

Put the roasting tin on top of the stove, heat the reserved 2 tablespoons fat, add the wine and reduce to 3 tablespoons. Add the flour, stir well until there are no more flecks of white, then pour in the stock or water. Stir constantly over low heat until the mixture boils. Season with salt and pepper. Strain into a clean saucepan if necessary, reheat and serve.

# gravy

**This is a thickened gravy for beef which should lightly coat the meat and vegetables.**

1 tablespoon fat from the pan

1 onion, thinly sliced

250 ml good beef stock

2 teaspoons cornflour, mixed with 2 teaspoons cold water

sea salt and freshly ground black pepper

**serves 4–6**

Put the roasting tin on top of the stove, heat the reserved 1 tablespoon fat, add the onion and cook slowly over low heat until browned, about 30 minutes. Do not let burn. Add the stock and cornflour mixture, then season to taste with salt and pepper. Stir constantly over low heat until the mixture boils and simmer for a couple of minutes. Strain if you wish or serve as it is.

# cranberry relish

100 g fresh cranberries

100 ml cider vinegar

about 3 cm fresh ginger, grated

½ cinnamon stick

2 juniper berries, crushed

2 cloves

50 g demerara sugar

**makes about 250 ml**

Pick over the cranberries and put them in a saucepan. Add the vinegar, ginger, cinnamon, juniper berries and cloves and simmer until the berries begin to break, adding water if it looks like drying out.

Add the sugar and cook for about 20 minutes more. Remove the cloves and cinnamon stick. Check the consistency – it should be like a loose jam. If not, simmer a little longer.

# cherry salsa

2 tablespoons sugar

200 ml red wine

50 ml balsamic vinegar

500 g cherries, pitted

**serves 4**

Put the sugar, red wine and balsamic vinegar in a saucepan and heat until the sugar has dissolved.

Add the cherries and simmer gently for 1 hour or until the juice has reduced to at least a quarter of its original volume. Remove from the heat and let cool.

Using a slotted spoon, transfer the cherries to a small bowl and serve. Discard the juice.

# salsa verde

1 tablespoon chopped fresh chives

1 tablespoon chopped fresh coriander

1 tablespoon chopped fresh flat leaf parsley

1 tablespoon grated fresh ginger

at least 20 sorrel leaves, sliced

freshly squeezed juice of $\frac{1}{2}$ lemon

2 tablespoons olive oil

$\frac{1}{2}$ teaspoon salt

**serves 4**

Mix all ingredients together in a bowl and warm in a microwave on HIGH/100 per cent for 10 seconds. Serve warm.

# romesco sauce

2 red peppers

100 ml olive oil

2 garlic cloves

1 fresh red chilli, deseeded and sliced

200g canned plum tomatoes

25 ml red wine vinegar

1 tablespoon ground hazelnuts

1 tablespoon ground almonds

1 teaspoon salt

**serves 4**

Char the peppers under the grill, put in a paper bag, seal and let steam for 10 minutes. Remove the skin, seeds and membranes. Heat 1 teaspoon of the oil in a non-stick pan, lightly brown the garlic, then add the chilli and tomatoes. Dry out the mixture over high heat so it starts to fry and even brown a little. Transfer to a blender, add the vinegar and remaining oil, and purée until smooth. Stir in the nuts to thicken the sauce and add salt to taste.

# to serve with pork, goose or duck

Rich roasts, such as pork, goose or duck, are traditionally served with accompaniments that are both sweet and sour. They used to be popular wintertime celebration dishes, so seasonal or stored ingredients were used. Cabbage is a winter crop, and apples were stored in racks for winter use. The apples and prunes used to stuff the goose are sometimes too fatty to eat, so these prune-stuffed roast apples are an alternative.

## danish red cabbage

1 red cabbage, about 1.5 kg

50 g unsalted butter, plus 1 tablespoon extra

1 tablespoon sugar

freshly squeezed juice of ½ lemon
or 1 tablespoon vinegar

125 ml cherry or blackcurrant juice

**serves 4**

Cut the cabbage into quarters. Remove the stem and shred the leaves finely.

Melt the butter in a large saucepan, stir in the sugar over gentle heat, add lemon juice or vinegar and half the fruit juice and bring to the boil. Add the cabbage and turn in the liquid. Cover and steam until tender, about 2 hours, stirring frequently and adding more juice if necessary.

Remove the lid for the last 15 minutes, then add a lump of butter and extra lemon juice if the cabbage is too sweet. Sometimes, a few caraway seeds or apple slices are added too.

## roast stuffed apples

4 small Bramley or other sour cooking apples

16 Agen prunes, cooked and pitted

¼ teaspoon ground cinnamon

4 teaspoons unsalted butter, melted

olive or sunflower oil, for brushing

**serves 4**

Core the apples, then make a shallow cut around the 'equators' so they don't explode in the oven. Brush oil over the skins with a pastry brush. Stuff each core with a cooked prune. Sprinkle with the cinnamon and push 1 teaspoon butter into each hole. Bake in a preheated oven at 160–180°C (325–350°F) Gas 3–4 for 50 minutes–1 hour until the apples are tender but still keep their shape.

# to serve with roast turkey

I believe it is all the extras traditionally served with a roast turkey that turn it into a feast, as well as making the bird 'go further' for what is often a very large family gathering. All these accompaniments can be cooked during the time the cooked turkey is resting in a warm place.

## chipolatas

Chipolatas come in as many varieties as regular sausages, but look more appetizing to serve as garnishes. They are often used to add extra filling to make an expensive dish go further, so allow at least two per person, and occasionally four.

2–4 chipolatas (venison if possible), per person
1 tablespoon cooking fat from the turkey

**2–4 per person**

Put the sausages in a small roasting tin, add the oil and turn to coat. Roast while the turkey is resting in a preheated oven at 200°C (400°F) Gas 6 until brown on one side. Turn them over and cook the other side. The total cooking time should be about 10 minutes.

## sausage meat patties

75–150 g fresh sausagemeat per person
plain flour, for dusting
olive oil, for frying

**2–3 patties per person**

Take portions of the sausage meat about 1½ tablespoons each and roll into balls. Flatten them between your palms, then put on a clean work surface and dust with flour on both sides.

Heat the olive oil in a large frying pan, add the patties, spaced well apart, and in batches if necessary. Fry until brown and crisp on one side, then turn them over and brown the other side, about 5 minutes in total.

## bacon rolls

rindless bacon slices, preferably smoked streaky (see serving quantities)

*metal skewers*

**6 slices bacon serves 2 people**

Cut the bacon slices in half crossways. Roll the bacon up tightly into rolls and spear them on metal skewers – 6 per skewer. Roast in a preheated oven at 200°C (400°F) Gas 6 for 5 minutes, at the same time as the chipolatas.

# to serve with roast beef

Yorkshire pudding used to be served at the beginning of the meal to fill people up and make the meat 'go further'. These days, it acts as a mop for the gravy and pan juices. If you're lucky enough to have leftovers, they are delicious next day with bacon for breakfast. Fresh horseradish sauce is an eye-opener in more ways than one. However, once you've made it yourself, the bottled variety will never be good enough.

## horseradish sauce

**Grating the horseradish will make your eyes water, but the result is worth it.**

1 large horseradish root
1 tablespoon white wine vinegar
250 ml double cream
sea salt

**makes about 500–600 ml, serves 6–8**

Scrape the fresh horseradish root clean and grate it finely to give 2 tablespoons.

Put in a bowl, add the vinegar and salt and stir well. Add the cream and whisk until it becomes thick and light. Rest it at room temperature for at least 2 hours, but serve the same day.

## yorkshire pudding

275 ml milk
2 whole eggs
125 g plain flour
½ teaspoon salt
4–6 tablespoons fat from the roasting tin

*a small roasting tin, 45 x 30 mm, a 6-hole Yorkshire pudding tray, or a 12-hole bun tin*

**serves 6**

Put the milk, eggs, flour and salt in a bowl and whisk well.

Heat the fat on top of the stove in one large tin or divide between 6-holes (1 tablespoon fat each) or 12-holes (½ teaspoon fat). Pour in the batter (take care because it will spatter).

Cook in a preheated oven at 230°C (450°F) Gas 8 until well risen (35 minutes for the large tin or 15 minutes for the individual tins). Serve as soon as possible.

# roasting know-how

It is useful to follow a routine when you prepare meat and poultry for roasting:

• Weigh the roast if necessary and calculate the cooking time, using either the tables for roasting (page 133, 135) or by following the times given in the recipe. If you're buying from a supermarket or similar source, the weight will be given on the packaging. If the meat or poultry contains a stuffing, that must be included in the total weight.

• Remove the roast from the refrigerator and let it return to room temperature at least 30 minutes before cooking.

• At the same time, set the oven to the starting heat (some ovens can take up to 20 minutes to preheat). Check the temperature with an oven thermometer (many ovens are inaccurate).

• If the butcher has not already done so, the meat or bird should be trimmed and tied if necessary. Extra fat, such as pork fat, can be wrapped around very lean roasts, such as pheasants or lean beef, and tied with kitchen string to keep it in place.

• If cooking pork with crackling, score the skin into strips with a sharp knife. Alternatively, ask the butcher to do this for you when you buy it.

• Baste the meat with the chosen oil, butter or other fat to prevent the flesh or skin from drying out.

• Season with salt, pepper or seasoned flour as appropriate. This is optional – some people prefer not to season until later (or even at all).

• Put the roast directly in a roasting tin or, if there is going to be a lot of fat produced (as with duck or goose), set it on a rack in the tin so it doesn't fry in its own dripping. This will also let air circulate around the roast.

There is an ongoing debate as to whether roasting at high temperatures for a comparatively short time gives a better result than roasting at a lower temperature for a longer time with a couple of short high-temperature episodes at the start or finish of the cooking. There are cooks who swear by one method or the other, but in my opinion both methods have their pros and cons.

## Fast-roasting

Only very tender cuts of meat are cooked at high temperatures. High heat shrinks meat fibres and toughens them, so anything that requires heat to tenderize it must opt for slow-roasting. At high temperatures, accurate timing is essential to reach the required internal temperature, whereas when cooking at a low temperature 10 minutes either way makes little difference.

If we look closely at the effect of a really hot oven – 230°C (450°F) Gas 8 – on a roast, it will show the internal juices being drawn to the surface where they evaporate, leaving a delicious concentrated coating on the outer surface. Inside, there is an edging of hot, well-cooked meat surrounding a mass of raw flesh in the centre and at this point, if the meat is 'rested' in a warm environment, such as a gentle plate-warming area, given time, the juices will redistribute themselves and the meat will be an even, rosy colour right through. This is an ideal way to cook meat to be served rare.

If left longer in the hot oven instead of being rested, the meat becomes progressively more cooked, drier and tougher, while the outside becomes seared, crusty and, finally, charred. The internal temperature of meat continues to rise for a further 10 minutes or so after a high-roasted cut has been taken out of the oven, which is why the resting period is so important and a lot of thought has to be given to timing with this method. It is easier to produce the required doneness when the cooking takes place at a low temperature. Typically this is at 160°C (325°F) Gas 3.

## Slow-roasting

Cooking for a long time at a low temperature suits the less tender or drier pieces of meat. It allows the gelatinous, connective tissues time to soften and dissolve, giving a rich, succulent texture and, since there is less shrinkage, the juices are retained inside without much loss of weight. Because this method of cooking leaves the meat with a braised or boiled look, the surface is often browned all over in a pan on top of the stove first, to give it a roasted appearance. Alternatively, it can be given a quick blast of heat for the last 15 minutes to give the same effect. This meat can be timed to be served either rare or well-done.

Slow roasts benefit from being cooked with vegetables packed around. They supply moisture, absorb meat juices and prevent the roast from drying out. Water, wine or stock is often added as well.

## Basting

Basting means to spoon or brush the roast with melted butter, oil, pan juices or stock. It adds flavour and colour and keeps the food from drying out. However fatty roasts, when cooked with the fat side up, such as pork with crackling, do not need to be basted. A bulb baster (page 130) can also be used for basting, or for drawing fat or juices out of the roasting tin.

When the breast of poultry or the tips of the drumsticks are protected with greased paper or kitchen foil, it must be removed from time to time so the skin can be basted to keep it from drying out and becoming leathery.

## On or off the bone?

Bones in meat, fish or poultry act as a frame to stop shrinkage during cooking and will give a looser texture when carved. If the meat breaks away from the bone during cooking or has been deboned, it shrinks and becomes close-textured, even tougher. Bones conduct heat, and so a bone-in roast will cook faster than a boneless one. They also contribute flavour to the dish, so even if a roast has been deboned, those bones are often used under the meat, acting as a makeshift rack, and adding their flavour to the pan juices. A boned-out cut will usually have to be tied into shape, producing a much denser cut. A roast with the bones in to provide structure will often be more tender than a boneless one.

## Up on a rack

Poultry, such as duck and goose, contain a great deal of fat which melts and is released during cooking. To prevent them from deep-frying in the fat, the birds are sometimes suspended above the roasting pan on a rack or trivet. This also makes it easier to spoon or siphon off the fat as it is rendered (retain it for basting the meat, roasting the vegetables or using on another occasion). Chicken cooked on a rack over liquid acquires a deliciously crisp skin. The liquid may be water, stock or wine, which can then be used to make gravy.

## Trussing of poultry

Poultry used to be trussed to make it a tidier shape. These days, birds are less likely to be trussed with the result that the heat can penetrate better, especially to the area between leg and body, the section most at risk of undercooking.

## Fish

Fish is best roasted at high temperature, because it does not need long cooking to tenderize it. Keep the skin on the fish to protect the flesh and give extra flavour. Some recipes recommend flashing the skin under the grill to caramelize it, rather like crackling. Otherwise, the skin may be taken off before serving.

Fish cooked on the bone will have more flavour. Depending on the formality of the occasion, it can be served as is, or taken off the bone for serving. The Chinese have a tradition that it is bad luck to turn the fish over during boning. Bad luck or not, you will find that it keeps its shape better if you serve the top fillets first, then remove the bone (snipping at head and tail with scissors if necessary) before serving the bottom fillets.

## Vegetables

Watery vegetables such as squash or tomatoes are best roasted at high temperatures. Vegetables to be roasted until charred to give a barbecued effect, such as peppers, courgettes or onions, should be brushed with oil before being subjected to a high temperature and then cooked more slowly until tender.

Root vegetables, especially potatoes and parsnips, may be given a preliminary par-boiling in salted water, to soften the outer surface so that it can become crisp and brown when basted with fat and cooked around the roast. After an initial burst at high temperature, root vegetables, if cooked from raw, rather than par-boiled first, will need further cooking with the temperature lowered to let the heat penetrate to the centre.

# fats and oils for roasting

Although most roasts begin their time in the oven with a preliminary brushing with oil, butter, or goose or duck fat, roasting is not in fact a fatty form of cooking. More fat comes out of a roast during cooking than is ever put into it or onto it at the start. The rendered fat is either poured off or taken off with a baster, and only a tablespoon or so used to make a gravy or sauce.

Unfortunately rendered animal fats tend to be high in saturates, but those from poultry, which are liquid at room temperature, have a higher proportion of polyunsaturates and contribute a delicate and delicious taste when combined with other foods or used as a roasting medium (roast potatoes being a prime example).

Oils can be heated to a much higher temperature than boiling water, which is 100°C (212°F). A higher temperature is needed to make the outside layer of food crisp and brown, intensifying its flavour while leaving the inside juicy and moist. Quickly browning meat in a very hot frying pan before cooking it in a low oven is a well known way of adding a 'roasted' flavour to an otherwise braised piece of meat, since browning can only take place at a high temperature – typically 200°C (400°F).

There is an upper limit to the temperature oils should reach. This varies from oil to oil, but it should not be allowed to reach its 'smoke point'. Not only is the smoke itself obnoxious, but any food in contact with it becomes tainted. Refined safflower and olive oils are among the best for using at high temperatures, because they have high smoke points, whereas butter and other animal fats have lower smoke points. For this reason, clarified butter is often mixed with oil, because it can be heated to a higher temperature. It should be noted that over-using and over-heating any fat or oil causes them to disintegrate and become a health hazard.

## Butter
In my opinion, this is the roasting fat par excellence. It is a pure, natural food and gives wonderful flavour to anything it touches. However, it does have a low smoke point and the solids will burn if it gets too hot. These will show as small black spots in the melted butter. They can be avoided by keeping the temperature low, or by using clarified butter (ghee) which has a higher smoke point. I would never choose margarine for cooking or eating.

## Goose and duck fat
These highly flavourful cooking fats give extra panache to foods cooked in them, particularly potatoes. The birds give off a great deal of fat while roasting, so there is no need to add more. Keep

pouring off or drawing off the fat as the birds roast to stop them stewing in their own oil. In fact, it pays to cook them up on a rack to avoid this problem. Both these fats are prized by cooks and are unlikely to be consumed in enough quantity to pose a health threat. However there are some authorities which suggest that the fat of water birds is one of the healthiest of animal fats, manifested in the phenomenon known as the French Paradox. This suggests that the people of south-west France, who have a diet high in butter, goose and duck fats (and red wine) have a lower rate of heart disease than other Western populations.

## Other animal fats and oils
Before olive oil was widely used in the kitchen – say the 1960s and earlier – dripping from the weekend roast was kept for frying during the week and for starting the roast the following weekend. This practice has now fallen into disuse not only because of theories that animal fats are unhealthy, but also because people are now more likely to use vegetable oils for cooking.

Since red meat fats contain a high proportion of saturated fat, these are not to be recommended on health grounds. However, every type of meat has its own individual flavour concentrated in its fat and from a culinary point of view, there is no way of substituting one animal's fat for another while keeping the original flavour. Gravies are of particular importance in this case and, although fat is often siphoned off or combined with flour before the gravy is made, it is the residual fat which gives much of the characteristic flavour. Fat found marbling through meat is a definite sign of quality because, unless it is a specifically bred characteristic, lean meat tends to come from inadequately or wrongly fed animals and won't be as tender as marbled meat.

## Olive oil
If you're going to have only one kind of cooking oil in your larder, make it olive oil. Refined olive oil reaches smoke point at 210°C (410°F), and unrefined at 154°C (310°F).

## Peanut oil
Also known as arachide oil or groundnut oil, refined peanut oil is favoured because it can be heated to high temperatures and doesn't have an assertive taste. However cold-pressed peanut oil does have a pronounced flavour. Peanut oil has a high smoke point of 232°C (450°F).

## Sunflower and safflower oil
These are both excellent oils, high in polyunsaturates and low in saturated fat, making them a healthier option than saturated fats.

### Canola and maize oil

Canola or rapeseed oil and maize oil are popular oils. My only objection to them is that these two crops, together with soy, have received most attention from companies developing GM foods. I would prefer to avoid them.

### Unspecified vegetable oil

This is one category that I would warn you away from. It is a combination of various oils, which are always highly refined. It almost always contains palm oils, which are almost as heavy in saturated fats as animal fat.

### Saturated fats in general

It is generally accepted that large proportions of saturated fats in the diet are heart and health risks. Saturated fats generally come from animal sources in the form of butter, lard or dripping, but also from coconut oil and palm oil.

### Keeping oils

The flavour of fats and oils is one of their most useful attributes, but it is prone to contamination and deterioration. The most usual damage is caused by leaving them open to the air, when they tend to go rancid. Sun also has a deleterious effect, as do moulds and bacteria which are encouraged to increase by moisture left in the fat after food has been cooked in it. So – keep fats and oils in a dark cool place, in a non-reactive, airtight container. However well looked after, they will deteriorate with age and should not be used beyond their use-by date.

Virgin olive oils last about 1 year, ordinary olive oils and other monounsaturates for about 8 months.

# utensils

### Roasting tins

Buy at least one large tin, large enough to take a turkey, but make sure it isn't too big to fit in your oven. Almost any kind of metal will do, but the thicker it is, the less likely it is to warp. On the other hand, don't buy something so heavy that you can't lift it and the roast out of the oven – a dangerous activity.

Buy at least 2 smaller roasting tins that will fit in your oven side-by-side. Use them for roasting smaller pieces of meat or poultry, or for vegetables and stuffings. Always choose a roasting tin only a little larger than the bird or cut of meat you wish to roast. If the tin is too large, the oils and juices will spread out too much and so burn too easily.

### Roasting rack

A roasting rack should fit your roasting tin snugly. If it isn't wide enough or stable enough, you may get your fingers burned as the rack slips towards you. This is particularly true of the kind shaped like half-cylinders.

Racks are used for very fatty roasts, such as goose, duck or some pork dishes, or even for regular roasts when people are concerned about fats in their diets. If you don't have a rack, you can use a bed of vegetables or bones to keep the roast off the bottom of the tin.

### Gravy separator

A separator is a clear glass jug with a long spout rising from the base, a bit like an exaggerated teapot. Pour the gravy juices into the separator – the fat rises to the top and you can pour off the juices from the bottom via the spout.

### Bulb baster

Invaluable for drawing off cooking fats and juices from the tin to baste the roast, or just to remove fat safely. If you don't have one, use a large tablespoon instead.

### Thermometers

A meat thermometer is the only accurate way of gauging the inner temperature of a roast. Leave it in for the whole resting period – the maximum temperature is often achieved only after resting.

There are two kinds. One you insert from the beginning of cooking and this one is widely available. The other, the size of a fountain pen (page 135, top right), is stuck into the meat when you think it's done and it gives an instant reading. The instant-read kind is available by mail order (pages 141–2), in kitchen shops, in some department stores and even hardware stores. They are very popular with professional chefs, and a wonderful gadget for the home cook.

If a thermometer is unavailable, test chicken and other poultry by inserting a skewer into the thickest part of the thigh. The juices should run clear and golden (press a metal spoon against the thigh to check the colour). If there is any trace of blood, return to the oven and cook longer until the juices are clear. Meats should be timed carefully according to the temperatures and timings given in the chart on page 133.

### Oven gloves

Use oven gloves or a thick cloth to take tins out of the oven. Never touch hot metal with a wet cloth – the water turns to steam and you can be scalded.

# roasting times

### Beef

There are two cooking methods to choose from when meat is to be served rare. First, it can be roasted in a very hot oven, then left to rest in a warm place. This allows the juices to redistribute themselves. It must be reheated for about 15–20 minutes in a very hot oven before serving. Alternatively, it can be given the traditional treatment. This involves starting the roasting process in a hot oven 220°C (425°F) Gas 7, then lowering the heat to 180°C (350°F) Gas 4 for the calculated roasting time (page 133). Allow 15 minutes per 500 g for rare meat, 20 minutes per 500 g for a medium roast and 30 minutes per 500 g for well done meat.

### Lamb

To obtain a crisp coating for roast lamb, rub the exposed fat with highly seasoned flour. Mix 125 g plain flour with 1 teaspoon salt and ¼ teaspoon coarsely ground black pepper and store in an airtight container. Add herbs just before cooking.

Alternatively, pierce the surface at intervals, insert slivers of garlic and sprigs of rosemary, then brush with olive oil.

Roast in a hot oven 220°C (425°F) Gas 7 for 20 minutes, then at 190°C (375°F) Gas 5 at 20 minutes to every 500 g for the timed period. If it is to be served pink, allow 15 minutes to every 500 g.

### Pork

This densely textured meat should be served without any trace of pinkness, but at the same time care should be taken not to overcook it or it will become dry and tough. The best method is to slow-roast at 170°C (325°F) Gas 3 without any high starting temperature – this results in a necessarily long cooking time of 40 minutes to every 500 g. Season the meat with salt and pepper as well as optional herbs or garlic before cooking.

If the pork still has its rind on, this must be scored before cooking to produce a crisp crackling. The oven temperature must be raised to maximum for the final 20 minutes. Many cooks baste every 8 minutes with the hot pan drippings, though I do not. Let cool a little before carving. Do NOT season crackling before roasting, though it is common practice to do so. Salt draws moisture to the surface and inhibits the skin from making crackling.

### Chicken

Before cooking, chicken should be brushed with melted butter or oil to protect its fine skin, then you can protect it further with either strips of bacon or a covering of kitchen foil. Remove for the final 20 minutes and raise the oven temperature to brown the skin. The cavity can be well seasoned before cooking with lemon, tarragon and/or salt.

### Duck and goose

Oven-ready and frozen duck are available all year and so are geese, although in spring you are more likely to find these frozen. Duck are usually 3–3.5 kg, while geese are usually 5–7 kg. Allow at least 500 g per person dressed weight.

Both are water birds and so have darker flesh than chicken or turkey, with a richer textured meat enclosed in a heavy layer of fat to protect them against the elements. This fat is much prized by connoisseurs. It is melted or rendered during cooking, then collected and stored for future use, such as roasting potatoes, moistening sauerkraut or other forms of cabbage and making duck and goose confits.

To prepare these birds for the oven, prick them all over with a sharp-pronged fork, skewer or larding needle, especially on the upper leg near the body. Stand the bird on a trivet or rack so the large amounts of fat can be drained off. This should be done 3–4 times during roasting, both for safety (so it doesn't burn) and to prevent the bird from being deep-fried in its own fat. To start the rendering process, the oven temperature starts high, typically at 220°C (425°F) Gas 7 (duck) and 230°C (450°F) Gas 8 (goose) and is then reduced for the main part of the cooking to 170°C (325°F) Gas 3 (duck) and 180°C (350°F) Gas 4 (goose).

### Game

The game listed here is all farmed game. For information on cooking wild game, consult a specialist cookbook. Only young game is roasted, because the flesh is still tender. The oven temperature is kept high throughout the cooking of smaller birds such as quail. Older pheasants may be cooked at a high temperature first, then lowered and cooked for a longer time.

Rabbit is better roasted in pieces rather than whole. The legs should be cooked for slightly longer than other cuts.

Venison should be roasted until just rare, then let rest afterwards. It will continue to cook and, by the time you carve it (after 10 minutes), it will be a uniform brown colour. If you cook it until very rare, then rest it for just 10 minutes, it will carve with a gentle pinkness. It is at its most tender served in this way.

# Meat roasting times chart

| meat | starting temperature for 20 minutes | roasting temperature | cooking time minutes/kg | instant-read temperature |
|---|---|---|---|---|
| beef  rare | 220°C (425°F) Gas 7 | 170°C (325°F) Gas 3 | 30 | 60 |
| medium | 220°C (425°F) Gas 7 | 180°C (355°F) Gas 4 | 45 | 65 |
| well done | 220°C (425°F) Gas 7 | 190°C (375°F) Gas 5 | 65 | |
| lamb | 220°C (425°F) Gas 7 | 190°C (375°F) Gas 5 | 45 | 77 |
| pork | | 170°C (325°F) Gas 3 | 85 | 80 |
| pork crackling | | Final 30 minutes at 250°C (455°F) Gas 9 | | |
| veal | Brown in frying pan first | 170°C (325°F) Gas 3 | 65 | 70 |
| chicken (whole) | | 200°C (405°F) Gas 6 | 45 | 82 |
| chicken (pieces) | 220°C (425°F) Gas 7 for 10 minutes | 160°C (325°F) Gas 3 | Total 30 minutes | |
| duck | 220°C (425°F) Gas 7 | 170°C (325°F) Gas 3 | 85 | 82 |
| goose | 230°C (450°F) Gas 8 | 180°C (350°F) Gas 4 | 40 | 82 |
| turkey | See chart page 135 | | | 82 |
| guinea fowl | | 170°C (325°F) Gas 3 | Total 1½ hours | 80 |
| quail | Brown in frying pan first | 230°C (450°F) Gas 8 | 10 minutes | |
| pheasant (young) | | 200°C (400°F) Gas 6 | Total 35 | 82 |
| rabbit (whole) | | 190°C (375°F) Gas 5 | Total 1 hour | 70 |
| rabbit (pieces) | | 190°C (375°F) Gas 5 | 20–30 minutes | |
| venison | As for beef, depending on cut | 200°C (400°F) Gas 6 | As for beef, depending on cut | 65 |

# roasting a turkey

A perfectly cooked turkey is brown and crisp on the outside, but juicy without a trace of blood on the inside, especially at its thickest part where the leg joins the body. This means that at the leg joint, the temperature must be 77°C (170°F), the meat juices run clear, and more importantly at this temperature salmonella and other harmful bacteria are rendered harmless.

For this to happen three things must be taken into consideration:
- the weight of the bird
- the oven temperature
- length of time per 500 g (1 lb.) used to calculate the overall cooking time.

Weigh the turkey and include in its weight any interior stuffings. Calculate the cooking time using the chart opposite, allowing plenty of time for resting the bird and dishing it up. Check the chart for oven temperatures and roasting times.

The lower the temperature, the longer the bird will take to cook and the juicier it will be. It is possible to cook a turkey overnight and finish it just before serving. However, unless something is done about it, the skin will not be a nice, crisp brown. If the oven temperature is set high, the time per kilo will be less, but there is a likelihood that the meat will not be cooked on the inside before the outside is overdone. So a compromise is called for – this is it. Start high, then turn the oven low for most of the cooking time, then high again (as in the chart opposite).

If using a frozen turkey, thaw it according to the chart. Do not let turkey liquid drip onto other foods in the refrigerator.

1 turkey, fresh or frozen and thawed

2–3 tablespoons melted butter or olive oil

10 slices of fatty bacon or 4 tablespoons butter for the kitchen foil

sea salt and freshly ground black pepper

*kitchen foil*

*trivet or rack (optional)*

**allow 350 g per person for an oven-ready turkey or 500 g per person untrussed weight**

Brush the turkey all over with melted butter or oil to lubricate it and season inside the cavity. Protect the breast and thighs with strips of fat bacon or a covering of buttered foil.

If the bird is small, put it on a trivet or rack. Heavy birds go directly into a large roasting tin. Put in the centre of the oven and cook for the calculated time at the higher temperature.

Lower the oven temperature to 170°C (325°F) Gas 3, remove the foil and baste the bird now and every 30 minutes until it is cooked.

Raise the oven temperature to 220°C (425°F) Gas 7 for the last 30 minutes or so and remove all protective coverings. Baste the bird well to crisp and brown the skin. Turn off the heat, open the oven door and lift the bird onto another oven tray to free the roasting tin for making the gravy. Return the turkey to the now cooler oven and let it rest and redistribute its juices – close the oven door to keep the bird warm in the residual heat.

Any turkey weighing 4.5 kg or less will need a minimum of 2 hours cooking time.

**Note** Whenever possible, buy organic or free-range chickens and turkey. Regular turkeys and chickens come from huge factory farms. Though absurdly cheap, they are pumped full of antibiotics and in my opinion have no discernible flavour.

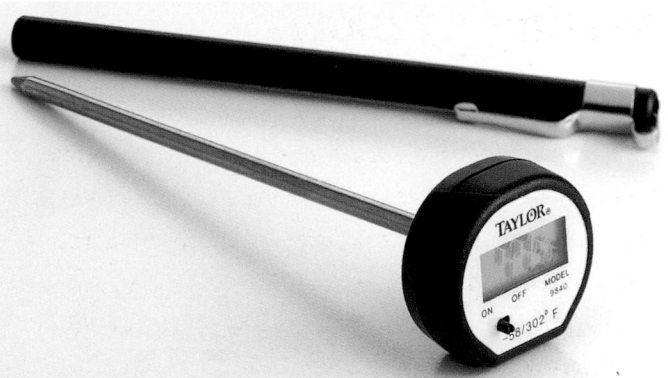

# Turkey roasting times chart

Allow 350 g per person oven-ready turkey or 500 g per person untrussed weight. Final internal temperature with an instant-read thermometer – 82°C

| trussed weight in kg | approx. thawing time in refrigerator | high temperature 220°C (425°F) Gas 7 time in minutes | basic temperature 170°C (335°F) Gas 3 time in minutes | finishing temperature 220°C (425°F) Gas 7 time in minutes | total cooking time/minutes | resting time in minutes |
|---|---|---|---|---|---|---|
| 4 kg | 65 hours | 20 | 140 | 30 | 190 | 30 |
| 5 kg | 70 hours | 25 | 165 | 30 | 220 | 30 |
| 6 kg | 75 hours | 35 | 200 | 30 | 265 | 40 |
| 7 kg | 75 hours | 40 | 230 | 30 | 300 | 40 |
| 8 kg | 80 hours | 45 | 230 | 35 | 310 | 50 |
| 9 kg | 80 hours | 50 | 245 | 35 | 330 | 60 |
| 10 kg | 80 hours | 50 | 265 | 35 | 350 | 60 |

# carving know-how

Carving a roast used to be the responsibility of the 'man of the house', and skill in carving was something a man was expected to acquire. Anyone would think it was difficult! It's not, and like many things to do with 'etiquette', the 'right' way is simply the most efficient way of doing things. Meats are generally carved across the grain, not because it really does make the meat more tender, but because the fibres will be short, and that will make it seem so. Some cuts, such as brisket, are usually carved diagonally, while the breasts of goose and duck are carved parallel to the breast bone.

For a festive meal, someone may like to carve at the table – and somehow it's always done standing. Have a plate shallow enough to let you cut all the way through, but deep enough to catch any juices. I think it's more efficient to have a second plate to receive the carved slices, and serve from that, rather than serving straight onto dinner plates. That way, you can share out the light and dark meat where appropriate. Even for less festive meals, a roast is still a special dish, worth carving at the table. Even when that's not possible, present the dish on a single platter – for example a whole fillet of beef ready-sliced on a bed of watercress or wild garlic leaves.

## GENERAL CARVING INFORMATION

• **Let rest**  Always leave a roasted bird or cut of meat to rest for 10–20 minutes before carving. During cooking, the juices migrate to the outside of the meat. During resting, the juices will redistribute themselves back through the meat. This will make it easier to carve and more tender to eat. Cover the roast with a tent of kitchen foil to keep it warm while resting.

• **Watch that fork**  Don't plunge the carving fork all the way into the bird or meat – it will scar the slices and let too much of the meat juices escape. Cut away from the fork where possible, so you don't accidentally cut yourself.

• **Add the juices to the gravy**  During resting, some juices will seep out onto the plate or back into the roasting tin. Use these to add to any sauce or gravy – they will add extra flavour.

• **How thick to slice?**  The more tender the cut, the thicker the slices can be. Therefore, a fillet of beef can be sliced as thick as a steak, but a cut like a boned and rolled sirloin should be carved thinly, about 10 mm.

# carving chicken and turkey

Chicken and turkey have the same bone structure, just as ducks and geese are similar, so the carving methods are similar. Chicken thighs and drumsticks are not normally carved into slices, unless very large, but the distinction of 'dark leg meat' and 'white breast meat' is still made. The choicest meat on both birds is still considered to be the 'oyster', which is found close to the backbone at the top of the leg.

When carving smaller birds, simply cut them in half, through the breastbone and backbone.

**1** Set the chicken with the breast up and the vent facing towards you. Anchor the bird firmly with the fork and cut through the skin between the leg and the body. Bend the leg outwards to expose the joint and cut cleanly through it to release the whole leg joint. Set aside to keep warm. Do the same to the other leg.

**2** Turn the chicken around and pull the wing away from the body. Cut cleanly through the wing joint where it joins the breast, and slice the wing in half at the elbow joint. This is optional on a chicken, but necessary with a turkey. Remove and discard the wing tip if it has been left on.

**3** Carve the first breast slice lengthways as shown. Then either carve the next and following ones parallel to the first, or else cut away and remove the whole breast, set aside the fillet piece and carve the rest in thin, even slices.

**4** Put the leg flat on the board, skin side down. To locate the joint, cut down across the line of fat halfway between the thigh and drumstick. Turn the pieces over and serve separately.

**5** When carving turkey, slice wedges off the drumstick lengthways. Continue carving around the leg, discarding any thick tendons which may still be attached to the meat.

**6** Also when carving turkey, carve thick slices off the thigh, parallel to the bone, taking care not to include any gristle from around the ball joint of the leg. The bone itself should not be served.

# carving meat

**BEEF**
- **Rolled roasts** are cut across the grain.
- **Brisket, flank and other slow-roasted cuts** should be carved at a 45 degree angle.
- **Bone-in standing rib roast** should be chined by the butcher. 'Chined' means that the backbone should be sawn through along its length between the rib and the spine. When you come to carve, put the roast ribs down on the carving board or plate. Steadying it by putting the carving fork only into the fat on top, slice the meat away from the flat bone down towards the ribs. Remove the flat bone. There is often a thick yellow tendon showing, and this should be cut out and removed too.

Holding the roast steady with the fork, slice vertically down to the bone, using a slight sawing motion. When you reach the bone, tilt the knife to detach the slice from the bone.
- **Sirloin or T-bone roasts** – the eye meat is carved as for the ribs, but then the meat is turned over onto its back and the fillet is traditionally cut along the grain. Now it is often removed in the piece, then cut crossways into medallions.
- **Fillet** – when the fillet is cooked as a separate roast, the meat is cut into medallions across the grain.

**VEAL**
- **Boned and stuffed veal or boneless cuts** should be cut across the grain.
- **Knuckle of veal** should be carved in the same way as a leg of lamb.
- **Shoulder of veal** – carve in the same way as shoulder of lamb.
- **Loin of veal** – carve in the same way as loin of lamb.
- **Breast of veal** – set ribs down on a carving surface. Slice down towards the ribs and between them.

**LAMB**
- **Rack of lamb** should be chined by the butcher. As with beef, chined means that the backbone should be sawn through along its length between the rib and the spine. When you come to carve it, you just cut out and remove the bone. Cut down between the ribs, so that each slice becomes a cutlet. Three cutlets make a generous serving.
- **Leg of lamb** can be carved in two ways. First, ask the butcher not to break the shank. A silver clamp (*manche à gigot*) can be attached to the shank, then slices cut from the round side of the leg. If you don't have a clamp (they can be found in some kitchen shops and antique shops), use a clean cloth or hold the shank steady with a carving fork. Slices are cut in the same way. If the

leg is part-boned and perhaps also stuffed, this is the way it should be carved.

Alternatively, put the roast on a carving surface with the rounded side up and the thick end away from you. Stick the fork in the narrow end and turn the leg parallel to you. About halfway along, make a cut downwards to the bone. Cut slices either side of that cut, angled slightly towards the first. When you have a series of parallel slices, slip the knife under them and cut them away from the bone. Turn the leg over and carve slices from the other end, some of which should be parallel to the bone. Lamb is juicier when cut in thicker slices.
- **Loin or saddle** should be carved in long slices parallel to the backbone. Slide the knife underneath to release them and then halve them in length. Discard unwanted flank fat. Turn the meat over and carve out the fillet which lies close to the backbone at the tail end.

If the joint includes the chump ends, these are carved separately slicing across the meat onto the bone.
- **Shoulder** – put on a carving surface with the thickest part upward. Cut slices in a V out of the middle fleshy section.

**PORK**
- **Rolled roasts** are cut across the grain. Remove the crackling first and cut it into strips along the scoring lines. Pork is better cut in quite thin slices.
- **Leg of pork** should be cut from the thick end, carving down to the bone in quite thin slices.
- **Crown roast of pork** and other cuts, such as loin, which include the bones – carve as for rack of lamb.
- **Loin of pork** – carve in the same way as loin of lamb.

**HAM**
- Hold the ham by the knuckle and make a cut down to the bone about 3 cm from the knuckle. Cut thin slices towards the first cut, taking care not to cut yourself.

**DUCKS AND GEESE**
- Ducks and geese do not have thick breast meat, so you carve them differently from chickens and turkeys. Put them on a carving plate or surface and cut off the wings at the joint. Cut off the legs through the joints. Cut each leg into thigh and drumstick. Put a carving knife into the bird at the top of the breast and, working from the top, cut long slices of breast meat parallel to the central breastbone.

# websites and mail order

## SONIA'S OWN WEBSITE
**www.soniastevenson.com**
*Sonia Stevenson began her working life as a professional violinist, then became a Master Chef of Great Britain running her own Michelin-starred restaurant. Now she is a 'Flying Doctor' cooking teacher, running cooking courses in the Lot Valley in France and throughout Britain, especially in Cornwall. Check her website for details of her books, courses and press coverage.*

## KITCHEN EQUIPMENT
**The Cooks Kitchen**
Tel: 0117 9070903 for catalogue.
www.thecookskitchen.com
*Mail order company with everything you could need for roasting, carving and other cooking needs. Telephone for a catalogue, or browse online.*

**Cucina Direct**
PO BOX 6611
London SW15 2WG
Tel: 0870 420 4300
www.cucinadirect.co.uk
*Interesting selection of mail order kitchen equipment. Telephone for a catalogue or browse online.*

**David Mellor**
4 Sloane Square
London SW1 8EE
Tel: 020 7730 4259
www.davidmellordesign.co.uk
*Well-stocked shop with all the cookware you'll ever need. Mail order available.*

**Divertimenti**
139–141 Fulham Road
London SW3 6SD
Tel: 020 7581 8066
33–34 Marylebone High Street
London W1U 4PT
Tel: 020 7935 0689
www.divertimenti.co.uk
*Two shops in London selling a fine range of kitchen equipment.*

**Lakeland Limited**
Alexandra Buildings
Windermere
Cumbria LA23 1BQ
Tel: 015394 88100
www.lakelandlimited.com
*Huge range of high quality, good value, cooking equipment, including roasting tins and racks, meat thermometers, bulb basters and some hard-to-find ingredients. Available from their many shops and also from their legendary fast and friendly mail order service (phone for a catalogue), as well as online.*

**Leon Jaeggi & Sons**
77 Shaftesbury Avenue
London W1V 7DJ
Tel: 020 7434 4545
*Professional catering equipment, open to the public.*

**Nisbets**
Freepost BS4675
Bristol BS2 0YZ
Tel: 0117 955583
www.nisbets.co.uk
*A comprehensive guide to light catering equipment.*

**W.M. Page**
121 Shaftesbury Avenue
London WC2H 8AD
Tel: 020 7565 5959
*Excellent catering equipment.*

**www.ThermometersDirect.co.uk**
M.M. House, Area D
3–7 Wyndham Street
Aldershot, Hampshire GU12
Tel: 01252 328255 Fax: 01252 332700
*For a range of thermometers, including pocket instant-read.*

**Wares of Knutsford**
Household and Hardware Emporium
36a Princess St, Knutsford, Cheshire
Tel: 01565 751477
www.waresofknutsford.co.uk
*Good old-fashioned quality ironmongers selling a selection of kitchenware.*

## FOOD SUPPLIERS

### FISH
**The Fish Society**
Tel: 0800 074 6859
www.thefishsociety.co.uk
*Fresh fish including organic and wild salmon, smoked fish and shellfish. Next day delivery. Amusing website – look out for Al Caprawn.*

**Seafooddirect**
Tel: 08000 851549
www.seafooddirect.co.uk
*Home delivery of fish and seafood.*

**Wing of St Mawes**
Tel: 0800 052 3717
www.cornish-seafood.co.uk
*Fresh and smoked fish. Next day delivery.*

## POULTRY AND MEAT

**Cornvale Foods**
Station Yard, Melling, Kirkby, Lonsdale
Carnforth, Lancashire LA6 2QY
Tel: 015242 22420
Fax: 015242 22350
Email: queries@cornvalefoods.co.uk
www.cornvalefoods.co.uk
*Friendly and helpful, able to supply guinea fowl, rabbit and other meats.*

**The Country Butcher**
Tel: 01452 831585
www.countrybutcher.co.uk
*High quality and rare breeds meat.*

**Ellel Free Range Poultry Company**
The Stables, Ellel Grange, Galgate
Nr Lancaster, Lancashire LA2 0HN
Tel: 01524 751200
Fax: 01524 752648
www.ellelfreerangepoultry.co.uk

**Providence Farm Organic Meats**
Tel: 01409 254421
www.providencefarm.co.uk
*Organic pork, beef, chicken and duck.*

**The Real Meat Company**
Warminster BA12 0HR
Tel: 01985 840562
Fax: 01985 841005
Email: richard@realmeat.co.uk
*Ask for list of butchers who stock Real Meat Company products. Good source for rabbit.*

## GENERAL FOOD

**Graig Farm Organics**
Tel: 01597 851655
www.graigfarm.co.uk
*Extensive range of organic fish, dairy produce, groceries, fruit, vegetables and organic alcohol. Mail order.*

**Organics Direct**
Tel: 01604 791911
www.organicsdirect.co.uk
*Home delivery of organic food boxes.*

**Soil Association**
Bristol House
40–56 Victoria Street
Bristol, BS1 6BY
Tel: 0117 929 0661
Fax: 0117 925 2504
Email: info@soilassociation.org
www.soilassociation.org.uk
*Listing of organic meat, vegetable and other quality UK foodstuff suppliers.*

**West Country Organics**
Natson Farm, Tedburn St Mary,
Exeter, Devon EX6 6ET
Tel: 01647 24724
www.westcountryorganics.co.uk
*Delivers food boxes weekly nationwide, including salads and herbs.*

## OTHER INGREDIENTS

**www.mycologue.co.uk**
40 Swains Lane,
London N6 6QR
Tel: 020 7485 7063
Fax: 020 7284 4058
*The internet mushroom shop. A unique selection of products to delight everyone interested in collecting, eating, cultivating or just appreciating mushrooms. Based in England, but will mail most products abroad.*

**The Oil Merchant Ltd**
47 Ashchurch Grove,
London W12 9BU
Tel: 020 8740 1335
Fax: 020 8740 1319
E-mail: the_oil_merchant@compuserve.com
*Excellent quality olive oil. Mail order, retail, wholesale.*

**Cool Chile Company**
PO Box 5702, London W11 2GS
Tel: 0870 902 1145
www.coolchile.co.uk
*Dried chillies and Mexican ingredients.*

**Extra Virgin Olive Oils and Mediterranean Foods**
Tel: 01460 72931
www.getoily.com
*Olive oils and Mediterranean produce.*

**Fox's Spices**
Fox's Spices, Dept GF,
Masons Rd, Stratford upon Avon,
CV37 9NF
Tel: 01789 266 420
*Mail order catalogue for herbs and spices.*

**The Spice Shop**
Tel: 0207 221 4448
www.thespiceshop.co.uk
*Dried spices, blends and herbs.*